CAREER STRATEGIES

Thomas Clark
Xavier University

South-Western College Publishing
Thomson Learning™

Australia • Canada • Denmark • Japan • Mexico • New Zealand • Philippines
Puerto Rico • Singapore • South Africa • Spain • United Kingdom • United States

Career Strategies by Thomas Clark

Acquisitions Editor: Pamela M. Person
Marketing Manager: Sarah J. Woelfel
Production Editor: Peggy K. Buskey
Manufacturing Coordinator: Dana Began Schwartz
Compositor: Katia Zhestkova
Printer: Mazer

Printed in the United States of America
1 2 3 4 5 02 01 00 99

For more information contact South-Western College Publishing, 5101 Madison Road, Cincinnati, Ohio, 45227 or find us on the Internet at http://www.swcollege.com

For permission to use material from this text or product, contact us by
• **telephone: 1-800-730-2214**
• **fax: 1-800-730-2215**
• **web: http://www.thomsonrights.com**

Workbook ISBN: 0-324-01403-1
Package ISBN: 0-324-01400-7
Audio Cassette ISBN: 0-324-01401-5
Video ISBN: 0-324-01402-3

This book is printed on acid-free paper.

Acknowledgements

I thank Xavier University for granting me a sabbatical leave to pursue this project. I also thank my students who served as editors for **Career Strategies** while it was in draft form. They completed and evaluated exercises and helped me select the best Internet sites for each chapter.

The editorial suggestions made by the following reviewers also contributed significantly to clarify ideas in this volume:

Robert Insley, University of North Texas;
Carol Heininger, San Francisco State University;
Paula J. Pomerenke, Illinois State University;
Myron Yeaser, Chapman University;

I am also grateful to Pamela Person, Lynn Mills, Amy Villanueva, and Peggy Buskey from South-Western College Publishing, who supported my efforts to assemble a multimedia package to help students learn about career strategies through a variety of media, including text, Power Point slides, cassette and video tapes. Katia Zhestkova used her outstanding talents to create the graphic design for this book.

And I recognize the talents of Greg Ganger of the Xavier University Television Studio, who directed and edited the video, and Otis Williams, Erika Hand, Julie Clark, and Marilyn Clark, who lent their acting talents to bring the script to life. My greatest thanks go to my wife, a thoughtful and tactful editor par excellence, for her support and many helpful editorial comments.

Dr. Thomas Clark

Forward

For the past 20 years, I have helped coach hundreds of job candidates on how to be highly effective in their job search efforts. From feedback I have obtained from recruiters, managers, students, and alumni about how they found openings and how they communicated in job interviews, I discovered the most successful job seekers had two things in common: 1) they took charge of their careers by defining their employment goals and strategies for achieving them, and 2) they developed and nurtured an ambitious networking plan that helped them find the information they needed to compete successfully for available jobs.

If you have ever wondered about

How to prepare for the future work environment
How to set up a job network
How to find jobs in the "hidden job market"
How to overcome a fear of asking for people's time
How to find information about companies for which you would like to work,
How to sell yourself effectively in an interview and on paper

then this book is for you!

It will take you through the process of assessing your skills and talents, developing a networking data bank, preparing your marketing tools, and answering questions effectively. At the end of each chapter, you will complete exercises to reinforce important principles and practices. Among these are Internet resources which can dramatically speed your ability to find the information you need for a successful job search.

When you put into practice the principles discussed in this workbook, you will set in motion a process that has the potential to dramatically improve your ability to control your employment destiny—alerting you to more opportunities now and in the future.

You will have

 made contacts that will benefit you in your current and future positions.

 become better educated about the reality of finding and holding jobs in the twenty-first century.

 learned skills that will build your self-esteem, self confidence, and self understanding as well as the interpersonal communication savvy that will allow you to be productive in the jobs you obtain.

All of this will happen if you take the time to faithfully implement the simple, time-tested principles discussed in this workbook.

How to use this workbook:

⇒ Turn to the Table of Contents to see how the workbook is organized.

⇒ Scan CAREER STRATEGIES, reading the objectives listed at the beginning of each chapter and then quickly skimming through the rest of the chapter.

⇒ Write down some questions you have about networking and the job search process, as they relate to your situation and objectives.

⇒ Then read the workbook chapter by chapter, highlighting those sections which are important to you and which answer the questions you have listed.

⇒ Do the "Networking Exercise" at the end of each chapter to put networking principles into immediate practice.

⇒ Complete the "Think About It" exercises at the end of each chapter to test how well you have learned chapter materials.

⇒ Do the "Three Things You Should Do Before You Complete the Next Chapter" exercises to stimulate your thinking about how to plan your employment future.

⇒ Visit the www.careerstrategies.itp.com website to gain easy access to the links cited at the end of each chapter.

About the author:

Thomas Clark is Professor of Management at Xavier University, having previously taught at UNC-Charlotte, Indiana University, and The Virginia Military Institute. He received his bachelor's degree from Drew University, and his master's and Ph.D. degrees from Indiana University. He directed Xavier's award winning Small Business Institute program from 1981-1989.

He has authored numerous books and articles, including Power Communication and The Executive Writing Handbook. His articles have appeared in a variety of journals including The Journal of Business Communication; Business Communication Quarterly; The Journal of Management Education; Quarterly Journal of Speech; and Communication Quarterly.

Dr. Clark is also the founder and CEO of CommuniSkills, a national communication training firm. For over twenty years, Dr. Clark and his team of consultants have helped thousands of people in the United States and Canada as well as managers in South America, Asia, and Europe learn to write, speak, and interview more effectively.

Table of Contents

Chapter Three:

SELF ASSESSMENT: TAKING STOCK OF YOUR SKILLS AND TALENTS

Chapter Four:

YOUR JOB SEARCH STRATEGY

Chapter Five:

WRITING EFFECTIVE NETWORKING MATERIALS

Figure 1-1
A Preview to Career Strategies
The Job Search Process

Understanding why networking is the most effective job search tool

Why is networking the best strategy in the new work environment?

How do I know who to call for information about jobs?

How can I overcome my fear of networking?

What can I expect to result from my networking efforts?

Getting started: Exploring what you want in your next job

What can I find in my work history that will benefit me in my job search?

What are the career opportunities that fit my qualifications and job goals?

Ideally, what job would fulfill my personal and professional goals?

Assessing your credentials and qualifications

What qualifications do I bring to a position?

How can I demonstrate that I have improved organizations for which I have worked?

Developing a job search strategy

Who do I know who can be part of my networking strategy?

How can I use my network to identify opportunities and other contacts?

For which positions do my credentials present an outstanding match?

At which companies can I reach my objectives?

Writing networking materials

What written materials will I need for my networking and interviewing tasks?

How can I convey that my strengths and accomplishments are a good fit for the jobs I want?

Preparing for telephone and face-to-face networking

How should I prepare and practice for telephone and face-to-face networking?

How can I use technology, such as voice mail, to communicate with contacts?

How can I learn how to continually improve my networking skills?

Preparing for the job interview

How can I best present an accurate and appealing picture of myself in letters and resumes?

How do I answer screening interview questions so that I will project a positive image of myself?

How can I prepare for behavior based interviews?

Chapter One

Why networking gets results

The best way to predict the future is to create it.
Anonymous

The trouble with the future is that it usually arrives before we are ready for it.
Arnold Glasow

There is no security in life, only opportunity.
Mark Twain

Chapter Objectives

 **How a changing workplace requires new approaches to job hunting**

Why networking is the best way to find your next job

Understanding the principles that drive networking success

What you can expect from your networking efforts

We are living in a time of far reaching changes in the workplace. In his article, "The End od the Job," William Bridges claims "the modern world is on the verge of another huge leap in creativity and productivity." People who had never heard of laptops, fax modems, and cell phones ten years ago now use them to communicate without regard to time or place. They can order products from the Internet at any time, on any day. And they can send multimedia messages to others from business offices, homes, cars, airports, classrooms, and restaurants. The founders of businesses such as Microsoft, Amazon Books, and America Online, have become billionaires before they reached their mid-forties. Their success has given confidence to a new generation of entrepreneurs who see vast profit-making and job-creating opportunities in providing products and services in an increasingly "wired world."

On the other hand, you've probably read the headlines announcing the downsizing of major American businesses. Hundreds of thousands of capable workers who had expected to complete lifelong careers at such rock solid companies as AT&T, General Motors, IBM, Sears, and Procter & Gamble, have lost their jobs to "outsourcing," "reengineering," and "right-sizing" programs. These displaced workers have learned a hard lesson: you can no longer count on a lengthy career with a single company.

Experts predict that as we move away from labor-intensive manufacturing jobs and toward jobs in knowledge-based organizations, dramatic changes will occur in the way work is organized—that companies will focus on the work to be done, rather than on the 9 to 5 job. For example, as part of downsizing, large companies are increasingly "outsourcing" work previously done internally, leading to a dramatic shift in job creation.

Figure 1-2:
Jobs will grow most rapidly in the information sector

Information sector jobs include teaching, research, creative arts, public service, data processing, public relations, hardware, software, and web page design, lobbying, mass media, sales, accounting, law, psychiatry and psychology, telecommunications, social work, publishing, advertising, banking, real estate, television, government, consulting, and politics.

Today and in the future, the vast majority of all new jobs will be created by small companies. And work will be done very differently than it was in the past. There will be more part time and temporary work, more telecommuting and job sharing, and more self employment. There will be less potential for job advancement in flattened organizations, less security, and more pressure for improved performance. You will have to learn to live with employment uncertainty as job security and careers with a single company become a thing of the past.

If you want control over your employment destiny, you will need to do four things:

⇒   **take responsibility for your employment future.**

⇒   **have a clear idea of what you want in a position and what you have to offer.**

⇒   **be committed to lifelong learning so your skills will be valued in a rapidly changing world.**

⇒ **learn to market your skills effectively to prospective employers.**

The increasingly fragmented nature of the new work environment, with most job creation in the small business sector and more jobs that are short term, will require you to use inventive strategies to gain control of your employment future.

Probably the most important of those strategies is networking: the use of a variety of person-to-person, print and electronic tools to communicate to potential employers that you are the confident, self reliant, uniquely qualified, eager-to-learn, highly adaptable, team player they are seeking.

What is networking and why does it work?

To begin, let's answer some basic questions: First, exactly,

 ## What is networking?

Networking is a process through which you build and maintain relationships with others for mutual advantage.

Effective networks are mutually supportive. Members exchange ideas, information, advice, and support. When you need help in making a career decision, your networking contacts will provide you with suggestions and leads. In turn, your contacts know they can turn to you for help when they need career assistance. A network is something that can help you throughout your life; it is not simply a one-shot effort to help you find your next job.

 ## Does it work?

Yes. Networking has proven to be the most powerful tool you can use both to find existing job opportunities and also to have jobs identified and created for you. Recent studies show that two-thirds to three-fourths of all jobs found in the US were discovered through networking—more than twice the number of jobs located by all other methods combined. Importantly, most of the jobs uncovered through networking did not exist prior to the networking contact. They were created specifically to take advantage of the prospect's ability to help the company solve a problem or take advantage of an opportunity.

Figure 1-3

Networking: A Potent Job-finding Strategy
Percentage of Jobs Found

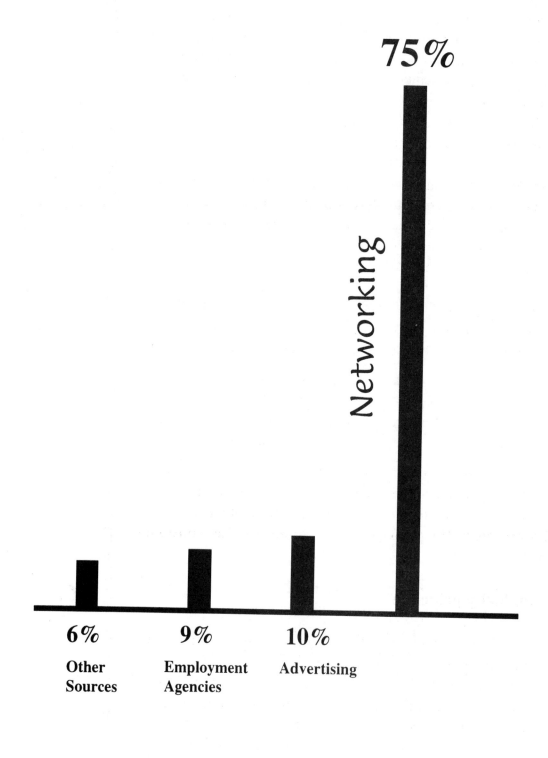

75%

Networking

6%

9%

10%

**Other
Sources**

**Employment
Agencies**

Advertising

Networking is a key to the "hidden" job market,

jobs that are never advertised and are filled only by those who know how to effectively communicate their skills to the right people at the right time. It is the primary tool you can use to find out about jobs before they are advertised in general communication channels such as want ads and Internet postings. In a sense the jobs are known only to a handful of company employees, such as the hiring manager, his or her managers, and the manager of human resources. This is a significant advantage. It allows you to make your case on the grounds of what you can contribute to helping the organization meet its goals. By talking to the right people at the right time, you can help shape the job description to match your strengths.

When you apply for an advertised position, you have to meet the criteria others in the company have developed independently of you. You probably will have a great deal more competition from all the other job seekers who have read about and applied for that position. Thus, an important networking rule is to find the job before it becomes open. Either convince a company that you have skills that will pay off for them or speak to employers about yourself so that when a job does become available, your name will come to mind and the employer will contact you for an interview.

 ## Why is networking such a good investment of time?

Networking works better than newspaper and Internet advertisements, employment agencies, and search firms because it reflects four laws of human interaction: **the similarity principle, the self-fulling prophecy, the principle of exchange, and the multiplier effect.**

The similarity principle

states that people hunger for close relationships with other people, especially those they perceive to be like themselves. Staying in touch with people who care about you is part of what makes work satisfying. In an increasingly impersonal work environment, many people welcome communicating with others who show a sincere interest in them. To capitalize on this principle, search for ways to establish common ground with your contacts, including identifying associations, interests, and acquaintances you share.

The self-fulfilling prophecy

states that people tend to do what is expected of them. When you ask for networking help, people are likely to help you if what you ask for is reasonable and within their grasp. Your task is to shape your requests so that your contacts feel both capable and comfortable fulfilling them. For example, in response to your first phone call, most contacts will be more comfortable helping you understand the opportunities in their career field than they would in recommending you for a job based on a single phone call or letter.

The principle of exchange

indicates that people cooperate with others when they believe they will receive something of value in exchange for their efforts. This may include a sincere thank you letter, a positive statement about them to others, and the potential of having a favor returned. In an environment of job uncertainty, contacts may help you because they believe you might be able to help them find work in the future. Good networkers are willing to give even more than they receive especially to those who have provided them with valuable assistance. Fortunately, with nearly everyone having e-mail, voice mail, and fax machines, you can efficiently share ideas, information, and resources with a wide variety of contacts throughout your life.

Finally,

The multiplier effect

demonstrates how networks of relationships grow quickly. As Figure 1-4 illustrates, your direct contacts lead you to others' contacts, who will lead you to additional contacts. For example, if you seek two referrals from a contact and get two referrals from each of those contacts and continue that process ten times, you will have made over 1000 contacts.

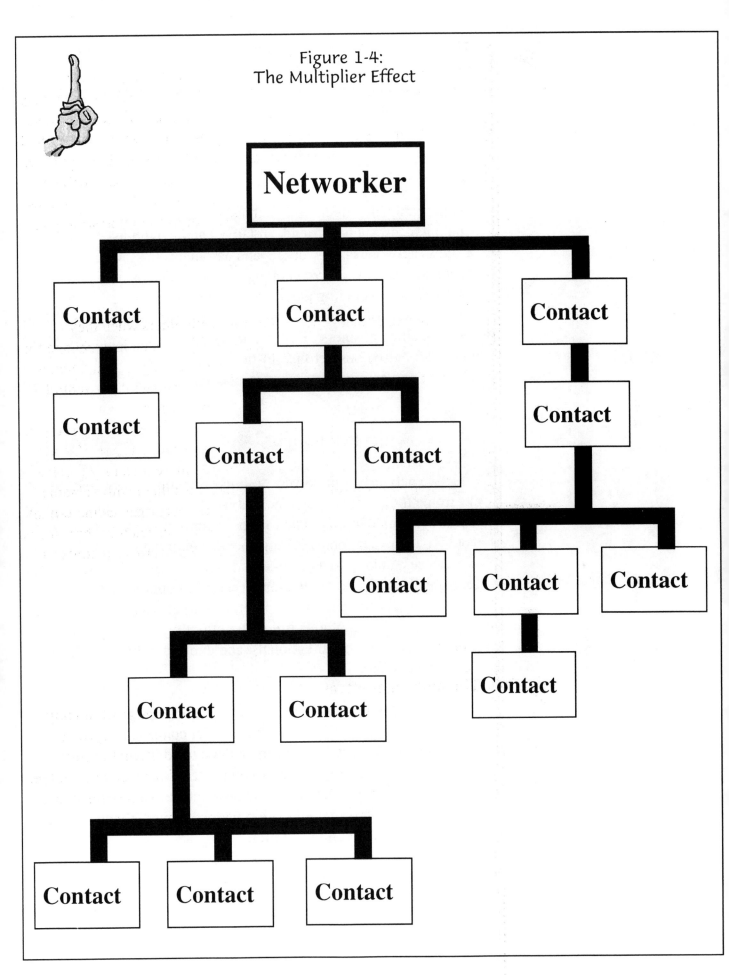

Figure 1-4:
The Multiplier Effect

When you network, you are asking others to open up their personal and business networks to you. As a result, it puts a burden on you to treat each contact respectfully and responsibly so that the confidence put in you is justified.

 ## With whom should I network?

You probably already have an extensive network of personal acquaintances, such as friends, relatives and neighbors, as well as a business network of co-workers and associates in service organizations to which you belong. Anyone can be a member of your network, including members of your church, social clubs, alumni of schools you have attended, and professionals with whom you have done business. Beyond networking with people you know, you should also consider face-to-face networking at conferences, job fairs, and continuing education classes.

 ## How do I network?

Effective networking involves a full use of people, print, and electronic tools. It is telephone and face to face meetings, and it is faxes, voice mail, e-mail, and Internet communication. Just as you would plan a vacation by asking friends about their vacation experiences, talking to a professional, such as a travel agent about your travel goals, and reading about vacation options in magazines, books, newspapers, and via the Internet—when you are looking for employment, you explore a full range of options: talking to friends, communicating with professionals, and exploring print and electronic resources.

You will find that networking can be done very efficiently in a computer-centered world. Networking records can be efficiently stored and updated in database management programs, and you can maintain consistent communication with contacts through e-mail, fax, and voice mail communication.

When and where should I network?

You should begin networking now, even if you have never held a full time job, even if you are a student or happily employed, and even if you have just landed a job. A good networking rolodex is the best job security you can have today. New positions and opportunities can open up at a moment's notice, including internships, replacement and newly created positions, and openings within an organization for which you now work. You should be ready with a mini-resume and a networking pitch because opportunity can strike at any time, anywhere.

 ## How can I overcome my fear of asking others for help?

At first, networking is hard work—it is not easy to pick up a telephone or to write a letter asking people for help in your job search. It may be inconsistent with your self-image of being a self-sufficient person who does not have to ask others for help to achieve objectives. And it can be discouraging. It often is not until you are into your sixth or seventh referral that you will find information that will help you find the right position.

To succeed, follow these three steps:

Request help that your contacts find easy to provide,
such as asking for job hunting advice or for insight into a particular career field or industry. While it may be difficult to restrain yourself from starting an interview by directly asking for a job, experience shows that to get effective help from others, you should design your initial communication so your networking contacts believe you are asking them for information as part of your learning process rather than as persons who can help you land a job. Once they have spent time with you and enjoyed the experience, they have an investment in you and will be more likely to take the next step and actually directly help you find a job.

Convince others of your value.

Highlight your most positive qualities. Indicate why each is crucial for a job you want—and give a specific example that shows how you have put that quality into practice. Focus on contributions you have made, such as improving sales, saving time and money, increasing productivity, safety, security, customer satisfaction, or reliability, providing needed leadership, and improving morale.

Be the person others want to help:

optimistic, friendly, reliable, honest, hardworking. To reinforce this image, smile, use a positive vocabulary, avoid apologies, take notes, dress neatly and be unfailingly polite. Follow through on all promises you make to contacts, send thank you notes, and return phone calls promptly.

How much time should I devote to networking?

Realize that your job search plan must be a top priority. If you are a senior in college pursuing employment or are unemployed, devote at least 15 hours a week to it formally, and more, informally. If you are employed, network by making it a part of normal interaction with relatives, friends, professionals with whom you do business, and acquaintances you have made through work. Even if you are happily employed, create, maintain, and cultivate your network because it often can provide you with information to help you in your current job. If you do lose your job, you will be happy you have a network in place to immediately use as a job finding resource.

What can I expect as a result of my investment in networking?

Networking allows you vastly increased control over your employment destiny—more opportunities now and in the future. It is a tremendous learning experience about the reality of finding and holding jobs. You will learn skills that will build your self-esteem, self-confidence, and self-understanding, and you will have made contacts that will benefit you in your current and future positions.

Networking exercise

Visit the Career Services Center of a school you are attending or have attended. It's usually the best place to get free, professional advice on how to investigate careers, prepare for interviews, and locate full time and part time jobs and internships.

⇒ Ask for handouts that list your center's print and video resources.

⇒ In the space below, write down what kinds of job placement, counseling, and interviewing services it offers current and former students.

⇒ Set up an interview with a counselor to discuss your career plans.

_____

_____

_____

_____

_____

_____

_____

_____

_____

_____

Think about it

Answer the following questions. In each case draw conclusions about what techniques work in getting others to help you and which do not. Then fill out the lists for what works and what does not.

1. Think about a time when you were able to persuade someone to help you with an important task. What exactly did you say? How did the other person respond? Why was your approach effective?

2. Now think about a time when you were not able to persuade someone. What did you say? How did the other person respond? Why do you believe the approach did not work?

What works in persuading people   What does not work

_____

_____

_____

_____

_____

_____

_____

_____

_____

_____

_____

3.   Describe a time when someone asked you to do a favor and you said "yes." How did they ask you? How did you respond? Why did you agree?

4.   Describe a time when someone asked you to do a favor and you said "no." How did they ask you? How did you respond? Why did you refuse them?

What works in asking for favors   What does not work

_____

_____

_____

_____

_____

_____

_____

_____

_____

_____

Internet references to bookmark

Visit and bookmark the following outstanding sites to read more about all aspects of career development:

http://www.Kaplan.com/career/ This is one of the Internet's best sites, including links on hidden jobs; resumes and cover letters; interviews; success on the job; and the "real world."

http://www.golden.net/~archeus/intres.htm contains a significant collection of articles on resume writing, cover letters, interviews, and other employment issues.

http://careers.wsj.com/ is one of the best Internet sites containing articles on all aspects of career development, including sites on Who's Hiring; Salaries and Profiles; Job-hunting Advice; Succeeding at Work; Working Globally; and Career Counseling.

http://www.jobstar.org/index.htm has excellent links on networking, the hidden job market, employment correspondence, and research on publicly traded companies.

http://www.westwords.com/guffey/site.htm is a very good site for a variety of business communication resources.

http://job.careernet.org/emphelp.htm is most valuable in that it provides good links to other sites.

Internet on-line graded job readiness tests

Take these on-line graded tests on the Internet to see how well you have prepared for the job search:

http://www.cweb.com/inventory/ Take this test throughout your job search to help measure your progress in job readiness. Record the results in this workbook.

http://cgi.pathfinder.com/cgi-bin/Money/goodnews.cgi Take this test to see how well you have prepared yourself for the future job environment.

Three things you should do before you read the next chapter

1.   See how the multiplier effect has worked in your own life.

Make a list of five people who are very close to you. Then list as many people as you can think of who were first introduced to you by each of these five people.

_____

_____

_____

_____

2.   See how people you know have found jobs in the hidden job market.

Ask five people who have been in the workforce at least five years if they received jobs that were not advertised in the newspaper— either jobs within the companies for which they worked, or jobs with new companies which they heard about "through the grapevine."

_____

_____

_____

_____

3.   Start thinking about what you want in a job.

Fill out the "What I find most satisfying about jobs" worksheet.

"What do I find most satisfying about work?" worksheet

To help select a satisfying career path, consider issues related to your personality. What has been most satisfying to you in your jobs, schooling, and activities? To help you explore this issue, do the following exercise. Rank order each of the following criteria, assigning a 1 to what most motivates you, a 2 for your second choice, and so on until you have assigned a rank of 9.

Challenge   _____

Opportunity to advance   _____

Money   _____

Security   _____

Friendly co-workers   _____

Professional atmosphere   _____

Demonstration of skill mastery   _____

Undemanding work   _____

Flexible work hours   _____

What do these rankings tell you about the type of work and work environment you would most prefer?

_____

_____

_____

_____

_____

_____

Chapter Two

Getting started: clarifying what you want in a future job

NOTES

Destiny is not a matter of chance; it is a matter of choice;
it is not a thing to be waited for; it is a thing to achieve.
William Jennings Bryan

To thine own self be true.
William Shakespeare

Chapter Objectives

 Explore your job history

 Determine what you find satisfying in a job

 Describe the ideal job

 Consider geographic preferences

 Evaluate other job issues

 Write a specific job description

Americans change jobs on average every three years and change career paths twice in their lifetimes. The average employee under the age of 30 changes jobs every eighteen months. So it is important that as you proceed in your job search, you think clearly about your employment future.

The most successful job searchers have a clear idea of what they want in a job—and of what they have to offer to hiring authorities. As a crucial step in networking, create a vision of your ideal job. Consider three issues: your role, responsibilities and activities that would best use your skills and reflect your interests; the work environment in which you can do your best work; and the pay, benefits and career path that best matches your career plan.

In this chapter, you will complete exercises which will help you develop a specific job objective, one which will lend purpose to your job search. You will analyze your job history, your work environment, and geographical preferences as preparation for defining the ideal job in the ideal location to meet your future needs.

Explore your job history.

To begin, brainstorm about your past jobs including titles, responsibilities and accomplishments; the industries with which you are familiar; and suppliers and customers with which your companies have worked. Consider all work, including service clubs and organizations related to your or your children's education.

Be sure to list the highest level responsibilities you successfully completed on the job—even if they were a small percentage of the time you spent on the job. If as an administrative assistant, on occasion you

⇒ managed the office in the absence of your supervisor,

⇒ trained people to use a variety of software programs,

⇒ wrote correspondence and

⇒ spoke to your company's key suppliers and customers,

write each of these accomplishments on your list. They help prove you are ready for a job with more responsibility and more pay! Also consider your personal preferences. What did you learn about what you like and do not like about a job?

Private for-profit organizations

	Small company	Medium sized	Fortune 500
Name of Organization(s)			
Its Location(s)			
Your Title(s)			
Functions: Jobs that I performed, including specific technical expertise Highlight promotions, highest level responsibilities, skills, knowledge, accomplishments, and recognition			
Environment: What I liked most and least about these positions			
Suppliers Location Name of Contact(s)			
Customers Location Name of Contact(s)			

Voluntary Not-For-Profit and Governmental Organizations				
	Voluntary Organization	Local Gov't	State Gov't	Federal Gov't
Name of Organization(s)				
Its Location(s)				
Your Title(s)				
Functions: Jobs that I performed, including specific technical expertise Highlight promotions, highest level responsibilities, skills, knowledge, accomplishments, and recognition				
Environment: What I liked most and least about these positions				
Suppliers Location Name of Contact(s)				
Customers and Service Beneficiaries Location Name of Contact(s)				

The next two worksheets help you use your job history to answer three critical questions, the answers to which are important for defining your ideal future job. The first, "For what jobs are you qualified?" helps you see yourself from an employer's point of view. The second, "In what type of work environment do you work most effectively?" examines your job history from your personal point of view. The third, "Describe the ideal job offer," helps you consider what is important to you in a job offer. This will help you define a job description that will guide you in your job search plan.

"For what jobs am I qualified?" worksheet

To help you get a better idea of the types of jobs for which you could best sell yourself, review the job history you just completed and answer the following questions.

1. With what types of businesses, organizations, or industries do I have experience? Include customers and suppliers of organizations you have worked for as part of your list.

_____

_____

_____

_____

2. What product and process knowledge have I learned?

_____

_____

_____

_____

3. To what types of companies would my education, experience, and proven talents make me most attractive? Why would I be attractive?

_____

_____

_____

_____

4. What knowledge do I have of the locations in which the firm does business?

_____

_____

_____

_____

Now that you have inventoried your past work experiences, think more specifically about what would be important to you in assuming a new job. Consider each of the following factors as you pursue this analysis, recording your thoughts in the space after each one.

Ideal work environment worksheet

Job requirements/responsibilities: Do you prefer a loose, unstructured environment where you are given significant responsibilities and authority, or do you prefer organizations where final decisions are made by committees or by a small group of high-ranking company executives?

_____

_____

Potential for advancement: Do you prefer a company where there are significant opportunities for advancement or do you prefer a flatter organization where can you deepen your skills in a single function?

_____

_____

_____

_____

Opportunity to learn or practice desired skills: What do you want to do on a day-to-day basis? What talents do you want to develop? Would you prefer to be the sole expert in an area or would you prefer to work with a team of experts? What kind of training and existing expertise would you like to see present in a company in these areas?

_____

_____

_____

_____

Co-workers: Will you have enough in common with your co-workers that you will enjoy working with them five days a week, eight hours a day? In your experience, do you work best with people similar to you in age, gender, social background, education, and income level or with a wide diversity of backgrounds?

_____

_____

_____

_____

Good stepping stone toward future career goals: What kind of hands-on experiences and responsibilities are important for future job you want to hold?

_____

_____

_____

_____

Company size: Do you prefer being a small fish in a large pond with a nationally famous company or do you prefer working for a small organization where you know everybody's name, including the president's? Do you prefer to develop a broad base of skills or to improve your expertise in a single area? Often smaller organizations are your best choice for a wide range of skills and large organizations for valuing and helping you develop a particular expertise.

_____

_____

_____

_____

Company atmosphere: What work environment best meets your personal work style? Do you prefer a fast-paced, high pressure atmosphere with multiple projects and deadlines or a slower paced environment where you may work on a more limited number of projects over a longer period of time?

_____

_____

_____

_____

Need for travel: Do you like the stimulation of extensive travel or do you prefer to stay close to home? How much travel can you comfortably accommodate given your lifestyle and family demands?

_____

_____

_____

_____

Values: Is it important to you to work in organizations where you like and believe in what you are doing? To work with people with ethical values similar to you own?

_____

_____

_____

_____

Work schedule: Would you prefer a flextime or an in-home working arrangement to a standard work week or an on-site job?

_____

_____

_____

_____

Ideal job offer worksheet

Job title: What title would you like to have? Consider how important a job title is to your self esteem. For example, is it important to you to be known as an assistant vice president rather than senior bank teller?

_____

_____

_____

_____

Salary: What salary is appropriate for your level of skills in the job you want in the industry in which you will be working? (This is an important question to ask of networking contacts who are informed on this issue.)

_____

_____

_____

_____

Benefit package: What benefits are important to you? Company paid comprehensive health care for you and your family? Child care assistance? Pension benefits? 401K retirement plans, matched by the organization? Tuition reimbursement?

_____

_____

_____

_____

Vacation policy: As time is money, what amount of time off do you want for vacations? What kind of scheduling flexibility would best meet your needs?

_____

_____

_____

_____

Perks of the job: Do you want a reserved parking space or are you willing to park in an open unreserved lot? Is it important to you to have a private office or can you work well in a bull pen or a cubicle?

_____

_____

_____

_____

Relocation package: If you relocate, how important is it to you for your new organization to help you sell your current home? Pay to move your belongings into your new home? Help your spouse find work in your new location?

_____

_____

_____

_____

Job Preferences:

As a next step, determine your job preferences. Analyze your job strengths and work preferences, as well as the advantages and disadvantages of each job. Make an honest appraisal. Evaluate choices first, then prioritize. Look at all past positions, voluntary and for pay, and determine what gave you the greatest sense of fulfillment. Look for patterns. Then make out a list of potential jobs and their advantages and disadvantages.

Top choice

Mechanical Engineer

Advantages	Disadvantages
*experience and expertise	*can get burned out
*excellent pay	*must continually upgrade technical skill or move to management
*lots of responsibility	*some engineers can be difficult to work with

Second choice

Technical Sales Representative

Advantages	Disadvantages
*large earning potential	*no industrial sales experience
*meeting new people	*frequent travel away from home
*pay based on performance, not politics	*sales quotas can make life highly stressful

Your choices, including pro's and con's

Top choice

            Advantages   **Disadvantages**

_____

_____

_____

_____

_____

_____

Second choice

            Advantages   **Disadvantages**

_____

_____

_____

_____

_____

Consider geographic preferences

For many people, a particular location may be the key to their happiness. The presence of family, employment for a spouse, a reasonable cost of living, good schools, safe neighborhoods, or recreational opportunities may be more important than securing the very best job that is offered. To help you focus your job search, answer the following questions about your geographic preferences:

 Are you willing to relocate anywhere or to certain locales only?

 Does your spouse have a secure and valued position? What would his or her opportunities be in a new location?

 How much are you willing to adjust your job requirements to remain where you are right now?

In defining the ideal location, also consider each of the following factors about the new area to which you may move.

New area

⇒ cost of living

⇒ quality of schools

⇒ location/climate

⇒ recreational opportunities

⇒ medical facilities

⇒ distance from home to work

Prioritize what is important to you in a job, rank ordering three or more attributes of your ideal job. Include these elements in your job description. Consider using the examples below as models for your job description.

Examples of specific job objectives:

A manager in a human resources department in a mid to large company in an urban Great Lakes area where there are good public schools and job opportunities for my spouse. A salary of $40-60K, with an opportunity to rise to department head. Ability to use my outstanding interviewing and career counseling skills. Good benefits including medical, life insurance, retirement and a flexible vacation schedule. Preferably near a large body of water where I can dock and sail my catamaran.

Merchandising manager for fashion industry in a warm climate. A salary of $40-45K with opportunity to interact with fashion experts. Preferably including travel to major fashion design shows. Full benefits a plus.

Buyer for career women's clothing lines for department store, $35-45K salary, in the Los Angeles area within commuting range of my current home.

Public relations manager for nonprofit organization in the arts, located in a large city with an established arts community, preferably in an area close to ski resorts. Salary negotiable. Outstanding benefits including retirement, medical, life, and disability.

Restaurant manager for fast food chain; potential to move into general management, $29-38K salary. Good benefits, including tuition remission and opportunities for continuing education. Near a major pediatric hospital, where my son can get excellent continuing care. Relocation expenses a plus.

Management accountant for auto dealership in Cincinnati area; salary 45-65K; preferably with a multi-dealership company. Comprehensive benefits, including leased car. Relaxed atmosphere preferred.

Piston ring inspector,1st or 2nd shift; within 45 minute drive of Detroit, $15-17/hr, medical and retirement benefits; strong UAW union.

My job objective(s)

_____

_____

_____

_____

_____

_____

To get the fastest results in your job search, be willing to accept a position that falls outside of one of your primary job descriptions. Once you have listed a primary job objective, consider other positions for which you could prove of value to an employer.

My alternative job objectives are:

_____

_____

_____

_____

_____

_____

_____

_____

_____

_____

Summary:

To effectively network about career decisions requires that you have a solid understanding of what your life's priorities are—which are most important and which are less important to your happiness. Then as you learn about various career options, you can better determine which options are in line with your priorities and which are not.

Networking exercise

Write down the names of five relatives or close acquaintances with whom you will talk about your career plans. People you know well will be the most approachable of your contacts and will make up the largest part of your initial network. They often have considerable insight into your values, strengths and weaknesses, and what fields you will likely be happiest and most successful in. Moreover, they have more interest in helping you succeed than networking contacts who do not know you well.

_____

_____

_____

_____

_____

_____

_____

_____

_____

_____

_____

Think about it

In the space below, based on your experience, fill in what you believe would be a description of the ideal candidate for the job you want. Then after looking over your job history, highlight your strengths and weaknesses in terms of the ideal profile. Think about how you can highlight your strengths in a networking or job interview and persuasively address your weaknesses.

Employer's criteria for the ideal candidate

⇒ **industry experience**

⇒ **product and process knowledge**

⇒ **management experience**

⇒ **level and type of education**

⇒ **knowledge of customers, suppliers**

⇒ **knowledge of a particular territory**

⇒ **willingness to travel**

Three things you should do before you read the next chapter

1. **Look at yourself through the eyes of one of your supervisors in a for-pay or volunteer position.** Record what you believe would be identified as your strengths. Areas for improvement? Important skills that you brought to the job and skills that you learned on the job? Consider asking these questions in networking calls to former supervisors.

2. **Make a list of questions about careers you are considering.** Develop a list of questions to ask networking contacts about the fields and positions you are considering pursuing. Base your questions on the answers you gave to the chapter exercises.

3. **Explore careers on the Internet.**
   Take three tests: the Franklin-Covey Personal Values test, the Birkman Career Quiz, and the Holland Career Test. Each will help you get a better grasp of the issues of most importance to you in selecting a career path. (See site addresses below.)

Personal values test

http://www.franklincovey.com/customer/missionform.html This test will help you clarify your values—what is most important to you in your life and how you want others, such as your spouse, friends, parents, children, and co-workers, to regard you.

Career interest tests

http://www.review.com/birkman This quiz will help you see what type of work is compatible with your personality and interests.

http://www.missouri.edu/~cppcwww/holland.shtml Similarly, the Holland career test will help you determine what career matches well with your personal preferences.

Chapter Three

Self assessment: taking stock of your skills and talents

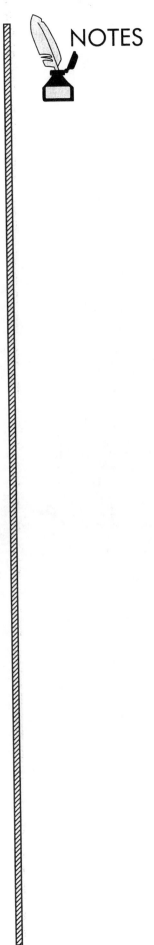

Success always leaves footprints.
Booker T. Washington

Chapter objectives

- ✔ **Develop an accomplishments list**

- ✔ **Prove you possess positive personal qualities**

- ✔ **Highlight specialized skills, skill mastery, and application of technology**

In **The Overnight Job Change Strategy**, Don Asher points out that when you are looking for a job, you should picture yourself as an entrepreneur with a product to sell and limited advertising resources. Your job is to convince people to hire you based on your future value to them.

Below are a series of exercises that will help you identify your usp, your unique selling points. Your usp is made up of the skills and personal qualities that are especially fitted to the jobs for which you will be applying. As you do the exercises, recall and record specific experiences from your life that demonstrate your best qualities. This will prepare you well for networking and job interviews, and especially for behavior-based questions, in which interviewers ask you to provide a specific example for every claim you make about yourself and your accomplishments.

To highlight the talents you have to offer prospective employers, write out three lists: an accomplishments list; a personal qualities list; and a technical mastery list. Writing these lists has three benefits:

- ✔ **They give you a fresh sense of the value you bring to employers.**

- ✔ **They help you develop an inventory of specific achievements to put on your resume and to use in your other oral and written networking and employment communication.**

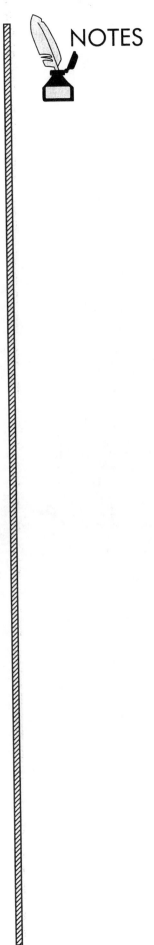

NOTES

They help you further define the kind of work you are most happy doing.

When developing these lists, show how you have used your skills to benefit prior employers. To begin, use the list below to help demonstrate that you have accomplished important goals for the organizations for which you have worked. Write down 1-2 experiences to prove each one. Find examples from all aspects of your life. While business experiences are typically the most persuasive to employers, you can also be persuasive describing experiences from voluntary organizations, school, and your personal life.

Develop an Accomplishments List

Focus your accomplishments list on results, especially those that helped your employer meet company needs. These include saving time and money, simplifying a process, and improving reliability, safety, health, security, morale, customer satisfaction, and company image.

 saved time
Example: I developed a computerized template billing form to replace our manual billing process. The new form shortened billing entry time from 3 minutes to 30 seconds, increasing billing productivity by 600%.

Your examples:

_____

_____

_____

_____

_____

_____

saved money

Example: I helped restaurant owners save $600 a month in laundry expenses by suggesting that they install their own commercial washer and dryer in unused space in the rear of the restaurant. The savings paid for the new machinery, including its installation in six months. After that time, the savings flowed directly to the bottom line.

Your examples:

_____

_____

_____

_____

_____

simplified a process

Example: I helped simplify the job application process at Americana Waterworks by consolidating three different forms applicants had previously filled out into a single form. This program proved to be a big success. It cut down the time it took to fill out applications significantly, and it also reduced the amount of paperwork the office had to file.

Your examples:

_____

_____

_____

_____

_____

➤ improved reliability

Example: I initiated a "start up verification program" to make sure that all needed plant machinery was serviced and ready to run for each machine tool order we received. This program improved our on-time delivery record from 65 to 95%, a key to cementing customer loyalty to our shop.

Your examples:

_____

_____

_____

_____

_____

➤ improved safety and health

Example: I helped improve safety and health at Covington Graphics by designing and enforcing a program that eliminated smoking in the workplace. Surveys we conducted found that the majority of our employees appreciated the cleaner air they inhaled, and our insurance company lowered our rates because our policy helped lessen the chance of a fire in our building.

Your examples:

_____

_____

_____

_____

_____

improved security

Example: I helped improve security at the candy store where I worked while in college by suggesting that we make three money drops at our bank per day rather than one. This meant that if we were robbed, we would lose only one-third of our daily cash rather than all of it. The owner of the company thanked me for the idea and implemented it at all ten of the store's locations.

Your examples:

_____

_____

_____

_____

_____

improved morale

Example: Morale improved dramatically at the telephone marketing company for which I worked when I persuaded my manager to let us dress more casually. As customers never saw us and only heard us on the phone, as a group, we did not see the value in dressing in expensive, dryclean-only business clothes. When I presented our case to our supervisor, she agreed, and everyone on the phone team was happy with the change.

Your examples:

_____

_____

_____

_____

_____

➤ improved customer satisfaction

Example: As a product development specialist at Juergans, I helped discover a shampoo polymer that was key to improving the product's sales by 10%. Consumer tests revealed that shampoo users found our product left their hair feeling brittle when dry. After extensive testing, I led a team that discovered a polymer that both increased the "soft feel" of hair and also conditioned the hair to make it more manageable. This innovation proved to be a significant consumer win that helped us increase our share in the highly competitive shampoo category.

Your examples:

_____

_____

_____

_____

_____

_____

➤ improved appearance of

Example: A proposal I persuaded the management at Chicago Autoworks to implement—that all our technicians wear uniforms to work—made an immediate impact on the volume of work we received. Prospective customers were impressed by the professional appearance of our workforce, leading to an increase in our business. The increase in business easily offset the $5 per week per technician rental cost. In addition, our staff liked wearing the uniforms because they no longer had to soil their own clothes at work.

Your examples:

_____

_____

_____

_____

_____

Other examples of ways you benefited your employer:

Consider all the ways you produced real value for an organization such as motivating others to do their work effectively, improving productivity, leading a team to achieve a goal, finding crucial information from external sources such as the Internet, using technology to simplify a process, or customizing a product or service to meet a consumer need.

_____

_____

_____

_____

_____

_____

_____

_____

_____

_____

_____

_____

_____

_____

Prove you possess positive personal qualities

In addition to demonstrating that you have benefited every organization with which you have worked, also search your memory for proof that you have exhibited the following personal qualities, qualities typically high on the list of interviewers' most desired personal attributes in a potential employee.

Goal setting:

Employers are impressed with candidates who are focused and have effectively organized their time to achieve short and long term goals. Show that you have planned to achieve challenging goals.

Example: I have known that I wanted a career as a special education teacher since I was in elementary school. In eighth grade I was paired with a learning disabled student to help her with her reading. It gave me a lot of satisfaction to teach her, and I also found her to be one of the kindest, most loving people I had ever met. I continued to be a mentor to learning disabled elementary school students throughout high school. In college I majored in special education and co-oped in a group home where I gained additional experience by helping a group of adult Down's Syndrome residents learn how to lead independent lives.

Your examples:

_____

_____

_____

_____

_____

_____

_____

_____

Problem solving:

Show that you are a good problem solver. Good problem solving can include analysis of facts to identify important issues, getting feedback from others, drawing valid conclusions, and developing effective action plans.

Example: I needed market research results from a colleague at work before I could proceed with a marketing plan, which I had committed to finish in one week. When I inquired, I found my colleague faced with a backlog of projects. He told me he could not meet our previously agreed upon schedule. So I worked out a plan to help him with some of his projects while he devoted time to statistically analyzing the market research data I had collected. He was able to get me the numbers I needed for my report, accurately and on time. And I learned a lot about the demands of his position, something which helped me in future communication with him.

Your examples:

_____

_____

_____

_____

_____

_____

_____

_____

Leadership/counseling:

Demonstrate that you challenge yourself and others to achieve goals. Show that others have recognized your leadership abilities.

Example: As head swim club coach, I directed four other coaches, two instructing older children, and two younger children. I told these coaches that our goals should be to make sure the children reached their swimming potential and that all have fun. At first, the two coaches for the younger children indicated they could not agree on a coaching regimen. One wanted a regimen of strict training, the other a more relaxed approach, with games interspersed with hard practice. I held a meeting among the three of us and indicated we needed to develop a plan which we would all publicly support. We decided that on Mondays and Wednesdays the kids would get strict training and on Tuesdays, Thursdays, and Fridays we would present a combination format. This system worked exceptionally well. In fact, the team rose to a second place finish in their league, up from fourth the previous year.

Your examples:

_____

_____

_____

_____

_____

_____

_____

_____

_____

Diversity:

Show that you have have built productive working relationships with people who differ from you in one or more significant ways.

Example: At a summer camp where I worked after my sophomore year, mixed within our largely middle class group for which I was responsible were four inner city scholarship children, who differed from most of us in race, family structure, and income. I set a goal of helping these children feel welcome. I planned activities that would give each member equal time and attention and would allow others to see them in a positive light.

I divided my children into three small groups. I asked each child to assign a positive adjective to themselves that started with the same letter as their first name, such as Tom Terrific or Outstanding Olivia. This exercise allowed everyone to laugh and relax. Then I had each child describe a positive achievement, such as helping others, an academic or sports award, or a volunteer activity. Last, after dark, we worked in teams to gather wood for a campfire, whittled sticks to roast marshmallows and hot dogs on, and told ghost stories while seated in a circle around the fire. As a result, the children got off to a great start together and became close friends during the camp week.

Your examples:

_____

_____

_____

_____

_____

_____

_____

_____

_____

Communication skills:

Prove that you excel at listening, speaking, writing, or reading. Demonstrate your talents at negotiating, deal making, or relationship development.

Example: I have learned how important it is to be an excellent listener, to, as Stephen Covey says, "seek to understand before I seek to be understood." When working as a first line supervisor, I found that many of the assembly line workers simply wanted me to know something bothered them and that I cared and would work to do something about it.

For example, one worker was upset because an air conditioning vent blew directly onto him as he did his job. When he told me he was getting a stiff neck from the situation, I listened carefully, asked him brief questions about the situation and the effect on his work and his health, and told him I understood why he was upset.

I asked him what he would like to see done about it. He told me he thought the vent's air flow could be redirected so no one would feel a draft. I asked if he would work with maintenance to correct the problem. He agreed, thanked me for my help, and the problem was addressed within two days. I learned in this situation that people are cooperative with managers who they know are interested in their work lives.

Your examples:

_____

_____

_____

_____

_____

_____

_____

_____

Imagination and innovation:

Demonstrate that you have used both logic and intuition to solve problems and recognize opportunities. Show how you have gone beyond accepted ideas to solve a problem or reach a goal. If you are in marketing or product development, consider discussing line extensions, additional markets, or new concepts you helped develop.

Example: I used creativity as a member of the Apartments House Council during my junior year at college. Our goal was to gain campus involvement from commuter students, students who often are reluctant to participate in campus activities because they have had fewer opportunities to get to know other students. I proposed and helped implement several successful events, including a t-shirt design contest in which commuters were randomly assigned to a team and met new friends as they designed and created "commuter identity" t-shirts together. As an added benefit, they could identify other commuters in their classes when they wore their new "logo" t-shirts.

We also organized a textbook exchange so they could purchase each other's textbooks at dramatic discounts from bookstore prices. This event drew over a hundred commuter students who both met new people and saved money at the same time.

Your examples:

_____

_____

_____

_____

_____

_____

_____

_____

Show that you have good work habits such as
good attendance, work completed on time, punctuality, honesty, cooperation with others, and support for management decisions.

Example: My manager at the supermarket praised me because I had perfect attendance all three years I worked there. She told me she admired my commitment and reliability—and my dedication to doing my job to the best of my ability. For example, I made it a point to be cheerful even when it was my turn to clean toilets or empty ashes out of the incinerator, the two dirtiest jobs in the store. I was committed to doing both jobs well because I knew they were essential to the health of employees and store guests and to the safety of the store operation.

Your examples:

_____

_____

_____

_____

_____

_____

_____

_____

_____

_____

_____

_____

_____

_____

_____

_____

_____

_____

Other positive personal qualities

Consider qualities such as integrity, loyalty, going the extra mile, and other positive attitudes you can bring to an organization.

Your examples

_____

_____

_____

_____

_____

_____

_____

_____

_____

_____

_____

_____

_____

_____

Highlight specialized skills, skill mastery, and application of technology.

Last, show that you have specific talents. Many times a talent you hold that other candidates or internal employees do not is the key to getting hired.

In the space below, write down all the skills you have performed on the job, such as running a CDC machine, using a variety of electronic equipment and software programs, or writing technical reports.

Over and above specialized skills that you used on the job, show that you have demonstrated mastery in other ways: this could include high grades; completing a licensing or continuing education requirement; passing the CPA exam; ability to speak and write foreign languages; ability to use scientific equipment; ability to conduct job interviews; statistical analysis; survey research; woodworking; web page design; or reconditioning classic automobiles. It would also include skills such as operations process analysis, process redesign, and production planning.

Your specialized skills:

_____

_____

_____

_____

_____

_____

_____

_____

_____

_____

Summary:

As job interviewers increasingly focus on specific proof from your past as the best evidence of your future performance, it is becoming more and more important that you maintain a journal of accomplishments such as those you recorded above. Then when you apply for positions both within your current company or with a new company, you will have a ready reference from which to prove your talents to hiring officers.

Networking exercise

Create opportunities to get credit for networking. Be pro-active in a class or a job in pursuing networking goals.

If you are attending class, propose projects to your teachers that will help prepare you professionally. These could include a paper or oral report based on an interview with a business, political, or community professional—or about a role model such as Lee Iacocca, Steven Jobs, Colin Powell, Elizabeth Dole, or Oprah Winfrey.

If you are working full time, write a proposal to attend a professional conference in your field. Show why the cost of the conference will be an investment in your ability to do your job better and how you will teach others in your organization what you learned to help them do their jobs better. While at the convention, learn as much as you can about your field and the trends that are affecting it. Network with the professionals you meet and be sure to exchange business cards with them.

Think about it

As you did in Chapter 2, analyze your ideal job through the eyes of a hiring officer. This time, using the lists you compiled previously, answer these questions. What accomplishments would ideal candidates for my ideal job have achieved? What personal qualities would they exhibit? What special skills would they have learned? If you are unsure, ask a networking contact who holds or has held a position similar to the one you are seeking.

Accomplishments

_____

_____

_____

_____

_____

Personal qualities

_____

_____

_____

_____

_____

Special skills

_____

_____

_____

_____

_____

Now search for examples that prove you fit the profile of the ideal candidate. Your strongest evidence will be that you performed a skill in a previous job or in a voluntary organization, such as school, church, or a charity. If you do not have direct experience, consider what you have learned in your formal and continuing education classes as evidence. Last, if you cannot claim a needed skill through experience or education, consider supporting your case by pointing out you previously mastered skills similar to the ones desired.

Accomplishments

_____

_____

_____

_____

_____

Personal qualities

_____

_____

_____

_____

_____

Special skills

_____

_____

_____

_____

_____

Three things you should do before you read the next chapter

1.   **Imagine that you have been offered the following three jobs. Which you would take? Why? Which would be your second choice? Why? Which would be your last choice? Why?**

A position with a Fortune 50 company with 60,000 employees worldwide. The position pays $39,000 per year, with full family health coverage, tuition reimbursement, a good retirement program, a voluntary 401K program. Some travel, including international travel. Extremely competitive, highly demanding work environment. Employees often put in 60-70 hour weeks. Limited opportunity for promotion. Many employees receive lateral transfers into related work. Good stepping stone for good jobs with other companies. Excellent continuing education offered. High potential for burnout.

A position with a small family-owned company with 100 employees. The position pays $33,000 per year, with limited health and retirement benefits. Exceptional level of responsability covering a broad range of functions. Friendly environment with a wide range of age and socioeconomic backgrounds represented. No travel required. Company has high retention level. Stable firm with loyal customer base and limited plans for growth. You'd be the youngest employee.

A position with a nonprofit organization with 200 employees locally. The position pays $24,000 a year, with full health and retirement benefits. Tuition reimbursement. Extensive training provided. Wide contact with the needy people served by the organization. Limited autonomy. Lots of paper work. Relationship oriented organization with some room for advancement, based primarily on education and seniority.

Daily local travel to call on clients.

2.   Take the EQ test on the Internet.

www.utne.com:80/cgi-bin/eq
The Emotional Quotient test includes 10 questions in which
you are to give your most likely response to a given
scenario. After answering the questions, your EQ is scored
and compared against highest and average scores. The
analysis includes a justification of the most mature response
to each situation. This website helps you see how a contact
or hiring officer might evaluate your personal maturity
based on your answers to their questions about how you
would handle an interpersonal issue on the job.

3.   Visit Richard Bolles' website.

Richard Bolles, best-selling author, gives pointers on
careers in his Web site, *What Color is Your Parachute*? at
www.washingtonpost.com/parachute

NOTES

Chapter Four

Your job search strategy

Discipline is the bridge between goals
and accomplishment
John Rohe

Nothing will take the place of persistence.
Talent will not....Genius will not....Education will not...
Persistence and determination alone are omnipotent
Calvin Coolidge

I use not only all the brains I have, but all I can borrow
Woodrow Wilson

Chapter objectives

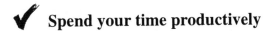 **Spend your time productively**

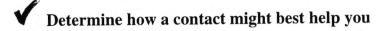 **Determine how a contact might best help you**

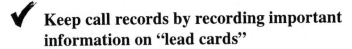 **Keep call records by recording important information on "lead cards"**

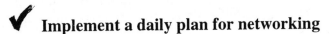 **Implement a daily plan for networking**

 **Explore traditional job search vehicles**

You are now ready to develop your networking database. Studies have shown that up to 75% of jobs come through networking: many of these jobs were found through a friend, relative or acquaintance. Others came from networking with former employers. And a surprising number of job leads come from "loose connections," people who did not know the job searcher well and who were found through a series of networking connections. In fact, a Harvard sociologist discovered that loose connections frequently produced better results than close connections.

In this section, we consider how you might best spend your time on networking, including some tips and exercises to help you network effectively.

Spend your time productively

View looking for a job as a job itself

Networking is a numbers game: the more contacts you make, the more likely it is you will find a job. If it becomes frustrating and calls are not panning out, remember this paradoxical rule of networking: As you increase your rate of failure, you will increase your rate of success. The more people you communicate with, the more likely it is you will find the one contact who will offer you an excellent job.

The key to networking is to identify all the contacts you can think of. While it is best to start with people in your field, network with others as well, because they may know people in your field or may know of companies that are looking for people with your skills. If you are in school or employed, consider spending at least two hours per week networking. If you are close to graduation or unemployed, devote at least 15 hours a week to networking.

Below, write down every name that comes into your mind whether at first the name seems to make sense or not. Make a list of past and present business associates, family, friends, church members, teachers, clients, doctors, attorneys, neighbors, bankers and accountants, insurance and real estate agents, past and present classmates. You can also find contacts at voluntary associations, such as athletic or country clubs, service organizations, and particularly professional organizations that represent the area in which you want to work.

Figure 4-1:
Expanding your networking database

To help you find names that might not immediately come to mind, explore old and new address books; rolodex and business card files; holiday card lists; company directories; files of company suppliers; customer contacts; alumni from schools you have attended; and membership lists of community groups you have belonged to.

Also check local newspapers for business meetings, trade shows, conventions and activities that reflect your interests and talents. Consider attending these to make face-to-face contact and to obtain a directory of the names, addresses, and phone numbers of all those attending.

For each name, see if you can establish common ground: people tend to trust people with whom they believe they share common ground. Write down ways in which you can show you are like the contact including birthplace, industry, job function, schools, associations, gender, ethnic background, age, religion, sports, charities, cultural activities and dress.

Determine how the contact might best help you.

Distinguish between informational calling and calling to find a job. Initially, it is typically best to say your call is a request for information. You might say you are looking for

 contacts with target industries or those who serve those industries;

 content and qualifications for target jobs;

 industry trends;

 job hunting advice; or

 agreement to contact others on your behalf.

After people have agreed to provide this information, they "have an investment in you" and are more likely on a subsequent call to act more directly on your behalf to help you find a job.

Networking list

Relatives, friends, and close acquaintances
who frequently can offer support and encouragement

Names	Telephone numbers E-mail address/fax number	Type of help	Common ground

Professional Colleagues,

including past and present co-workers as well as professionals you know. Bankers, accountants, lawyers, and consulting firms are particularly valuable sources because of their close contacts with a variety of businesses. Here is the most likely place you will find experts in the job search process and mentors who can offer excellent insight into their professions.

Names	Telephone numbers E-mail address/fax number	Type of help	Common ground

Service and political organizations

Names	Telephone numbers E-mail address/fax number	Type of help	Common ground

Teachers, guidance counselors

Names	Telephone numbers E-mail address/fax number	Type of help	Common ground

Church and social club members

Names	Telephone numbers E-mail address/fax number	Type of help	Common ground

Neighbors

Names	Telephone numbers E-mail address/fax number	Type of help	Common ground

Keep call records by recording important information on "lead cards"

Lead cards are the heart of your networking call system. After making out your networking lists, write each name and other pertinent information onto lead cards. They provide a record of your networking efforts including, on the front, important details, such as the name, title, company, address, and phone numbers of the contact, as well as notes on each communication with the contact.

The back of the card includes information which will help you establish common ground with your contact, including names of family members, birthplaces, education, careers, awards, mutual friends, associations, and the names of the contacts that person provided. You may also keep this information in a database on your computer.

You will find this information to be invaluable to you, especially as you make initial and follow-up calls to a contact, or when you want to send thank you letters to all the people who helped you in pursuing a lead. See an example of a lead card in Figure 4-2

Figure 4-2:
Lead Cards

(Front: business information)

Contact's Name   Noreen Ader

Notes on networking history: Resume and letter sent 10/30/99.
Follow up phone call, 11/03/99, found out Ms. Adler was in a meeting.
Called on 11/05/99, asked if resume arrived; it did; made appointment to speak with Ms. Adler on 11/12/99 at 7:45 for breakfast (my treat!)

Phone   973-876-xxxx (Home)   973-745-xxxx (Office)
Fax   973-456-xxxx   e-mail adern@ameriskills.org

Title   Vice President for Human Resources

Company Address: AmeriSkills, 2648 Little Road, Branchville, NJ 05443
Company Internet Address: www.ameriskills.org
Company Data: insurance, property investment company, $300 million/yrly sales
Name of contact referrer: Vickie Browning of Women in Communications

Figure 4-2 (cont.):
Lead Cards

(Back: personal information)

Names of family members: Bill (hus); Julie, 15; Jason, 12; Jennifer, 6.
Birthrates/birthplaces of family members: Paterson, NJ   Newton, NJ
Education: Fairleigh Dickinson University (high school)
Career path: started as human resources administrative assistant; attended
            night school; rose to vice president through consistent and loyal
            performance
Awards: Varsity letters in high school field hockey
Mutual friends/acquaintances: Vickie Browning
Connections (religion, membership, political groups, sports)
            Republican; strongly believes in equal opportunity for women in
            the workplace; deeply involved with local public school; soccer
            mom
Contacts provided: Erin Franz, VP Human Resources, Atwood Industries
            Ruth Jefferson, Employee Assistance Program Director, Mercy
            Hospital

Prioritizing contacts

After you have completed the above, use different color
highlighters or lead cards to identify the probable priority value of
each contact, as illustrated in Figure 4-3.

Figure 4-3:
Prioritizing Contacts

red   ability to hire (face to face interview. Send letter of
                 application, two page resume, business card, thank you note,
                 follow up calls)

blue   knows person who can hire personally or professionally
                 (face to face interview; insight into preferences of hiring
                 authority and the company culture. Send resume, business
                 card, thank you note, follow up calls)

green   works for a target company—can refer to person who hires
                 (telephone interview, get name of hiring authority; insight
                 into the company; industry trends. Send resume and
                 business card, thank you note, follow up calls)

brown   works in a position similar to the one you are seeking or
                 knows someone who works for a target industry; find out
                 appropriate career path; opportunities for related work
                 (telephone interview; thank you letter, resume, business
                 card, follow up call)

yellow   little likelihood of helping (mail resume, business card,
                 and letter saying you are seeking employment in
                 particular field/function and are also considering a
                 related field/function, follow up call)

Implement a daily plan for networking.

Each work day, write down the names of people whom you will call and plan what you will say to each contact. For example, you might determine as your first week's goal to make 5-25 calls or e-mails each day, resulting in 10-50 leads per day and a fresh set of contacts to begin calling the following week.

Begin networking with people who know you well.

This makes the process less threatening by removing many of the psychological barriers that may keep you from starting a networking campaign.

Find out the appropriate career path.

An early networking call should be to someone who holds a position similar to the one you desire. Find out how that person rose to that position and if that is the normal career path. Determine what skills are necessary and which, while not necessary, add considerable value. This will allow you to understand at what level you should be looking for a position in that industry and what you need to stress in your networking communications. You will also receive a "realistic job preview," finding out about the advantages and disadvantages of the job, and the personal qualities shared by the most successful people in that field.

Determine what an ideal candidate would bring to the table.

Ask what credentials the ideal candidate for the position you desire would present. Ask about past work experience, product and process knowledge, education, accomplishments on the job, volunteer work, and personal qualities. Also ask what related positions would be available to someone with these skills. The answers might help you find new and satisfying career options.

Find out what kinds of objections a hiring authority might raise about your credentials and how the contact suggests you respond to them.

These may include not having enough experience, having too much experience, having the wrong kind of experience, having too little or too much education, lack of knowledge of hardware or software, or lack of an expected certification.

Explore traditional job search vehicles In addition to networking, spend 2-4 hours a week on traditional formal job search vehicles.

Figure 4-4:
Traditional Job Sources

State employment service: about 5% of job seekers get jobs through leads provided by these agencies.

Local newspaper ads: a place for entry-level management, administrative, technical and non-supervisory positions; management and non-management jobs for small businesses that are not well known to the public.

Ads in major outlets such as the Wall Street Journal and National Employment Business Weekly: unusual combination of skills that need to be filled; high level executive positions.

Internet sites: many companies which have websites use them to advertise jobs. There are also sites such as Monster Board which advertise jobs all over the world.

Private employment agency: about 5% of job seekers find a job here. If you choose this route, select a headhunting agency which specializes in the type of work you do. Avoid companies that make you pay a hefty fee whether or not they help you land a position.

Sending resumes to personnel departments of businesses in your desired area: Previous research indicates it can take as many as 500 resumes to get one interview. On the other hand, if you write a particularly compelling letter, highlighting how you can help an organization increase its profits or meet other goals, you may land an interview and, if you sell yourself effectively in the interview, a job!

Despite what some books on networking say, many people, typically one-fourth to one-third, have gotten jobs through traditional sources. Competition for the best advertised jobs may be highly intense. This is because in advertising a job, the company has defined what it wants, and you must be able to show you meet their strict criteria.

Spend 2-8 hours a week targeting the companies for which you want to work.

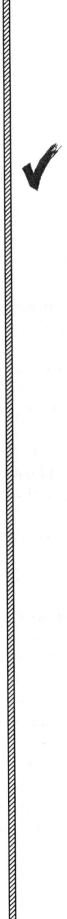

After making a number of networking calls to find out about opportunities for using your expertise, identify companies for which you believe your credentials are particularly suited. The following sources are especially useful for finding company names, addresses, and telephone numbers:

⇒   Yellow pages of cities in which you want to work

⇒   Chamber of Commerce membership lists

⇒   Trade press for the industry in which you are interested

⇒   Libraries

⇒   Career Planning and Placement offices of local colleges

Exceptionally good sources of information can be found on the Internet. Search engines, such as Lycos and Yahoo, will help you locate what a company says about itself, its products, and its services. Search engines can also help you find on-line bulletin boards and UseNet groups that can yield "inside" information often not printed on official company web sites. For a fee you can order customized reports on companies from Dow Jones & Co. and Dun & Bradstreet.

For individual companies, ask a librarian to help you find the company's annual report, as well as journal and newsletter articles covering the company. You can also call a company's public relations or customer service departments and ask for catalogs, brochures, ads, and other public materials.

For each company at which you interview, you should know some basic information: what services the company provides or products it makes; how large the company is and where it does business; who the company's key competitors are, and the company's relative standing among them.

Then focus your efforts on these companies. Write an impressive letter, call as a follow up, and request an opportunity for a face-to-face interview. Ask for a tour and look for answers to key questions. Is the workplace alive with energy or filled with tension? Do people look involved? happy? relaxed? tense? bored? Are people exchanging information or staying to themselves?

See if any jobs are posted on bulletin boards. Ask what the company sees as its key opportunities for the future. At all stages, be prepared to sell your strengths and contributions because you might just be in the right place at the right time. If it seems appropriate, offer to help with work on the spot to prove your ability and willingness to work effectively in that environment. After the tour, call some of the people you met. Assure them you will keep their comments in confidence and ask them for an insider's view of the company.

Also consider making contacts and learning employment techniques by joining a "job club" sponsored by a church or community group. You will hear lectures from professionals, get ideas from fellow members, and perhaps leads for your next job.

 Spend some time each week pursuing other important goals:

All work and no play can lead to burnout. So plan activities for yourself, including self analysis and self education, spiritual development, family interaction, and recreation. For example, if you are unemployed, you might develop an OGSM (objectives, goals, strategy, and measures) plan similar to the one below.

Figure 4-4

OGSM Plan

Objectives	Goals:	Strategy	Measurement
To design and execute a plan to obtain a position that makes effective use of my financial analysis skills while maintaining a healthy lifestyle and an optimistic attitude toward myself, my family, and the contacts who are going to help me land a great job.	To make at least thirty productive networking contacts a week. To learn how to communicate my experience, education and personal talents effectively for an entry-level position in financial analysis. To develop persuasive written and oral marketing messages. To maintain a positive commitment to mental, physical, family, and spiritual health.	Make a comprehensive list of contacts and write, call or speak face-to-face to each one. Read books & Internet resources on writing resumes, cover letters, and other job related correspondence. Compose these materials and ask others how to give me advice on how to improve them as well as other employment communication skills Do a thorough self-analysis; read books on interviewing, talk to career counselors and people who work in financial analysis. Execute a physical fitness plan. Ask spouse and children how we can make our time together fulfilling. Develop sources of spiritual strength.	Spend 20 hours a week on direct networking activities including meetings, telephone calls and correspondence. Spend 4-5 hours a week on traditional job sources. Spend 4-5 hours per week on marketing materials and networking pitches. Spend 2-4 hours a week reading resources that will help me understand trends affecting my industry and my job function. Investigate target companies or speak with employment professionals. Spend 1-2 hours per week on self analysis, such as taking and interpreting free Internet career tests. Take a fifteen minute break for each two hours worked. Have an exercise plan during which I exercise 2-3 hours per week. Spend a minimum of 5-10 hours a week of quality time with my family. Meditate each day on what is positive in my life.

Set up good records

To make the best use of the time you will be spending on networking, set up an effective record keeping system. Specifically,

⇒ Keep a copy of each letter you send out in reverse chronological order, putting each new letter on top of previous letters in a three ring binder.

⇒ File letters from contacts or potential employers in alphabetical order in another three ring binder.

⇒ Keep records of networking calls and meetings: you can use job lead cards, or if you have a computer with a data base management system, you can use this function effectively for this job.

⇒ Send thank you notes to each contact. You may want to set up model letters on a word processor.

Figure 4-5:
Supplies and technology needed for networking

Supplies:

⇒ a portable monthly planning calendar
⇒ expense log (job hunting expenses are sometimes tax deductible)
⇒ 4x6 index cards and 2 three-ring binders
⇒ high quality white stationery for resumes and letters
⇒ 9x12 envelopes that match stationery
⇒ three-ring binders

Technology:

⇒ word processor for changing resumes for each job
⇒ answering machine or service
⇒ access to fax, copying machines, a laser printer, and the Internet

Summary

As you begin your networking campaign, commit yourself to making out a schedule of activities that reflect important priorities: spending the large majority of your time on networking calls and meetings—and also investing time in creating marketing materials, targeting companies, practicing answers to questions typically asked in networking interviews, keeping good records, and planning to spend quality time addressing important social, family, spiritual, and physical needs.

Networking activity

Find out information about a company using one or more of the three approaches described below. Write down as much as you can about a target company, including the services the company provides or products it makes; how large the company is and where it does business; key company personnel; who the company's key competitors are; and the company's relative standing among them.

Internet sources:

Put the name of the company in which you are interested into one or more search engines listed below. Find out what the company says about itself in its annual report. Also enter chat rooms that discuss the company—you may find information here that you would find nowhere else. You can also often find news articles about the company which often will give you a balanced treatment of the company's strengths and weaknesses.

 www.hoovers.com

 www.jobsafari.com/wa.html

 www.jobsmart.org/

 http://investing.lycos.com/ is particularly valuable in finding recent news about publicly traded companies

Traditional sources

 For small companies, call area Chambers of Commerce and Better Business Bureaus. For a small fee they often will give you access to the information they have on member firms. These materials will allow you to know what industries operate in a given locale, the size of these operations and the names of key officers, information that will help you prepare for networking calls and interviews, or

 Check library editions of local business papers which often have an annual issue devoted to descriptions of area businesses, or

 Call Human Resources, Marketing, or Communications departments of companies and ask for product brochures, company newsletters, and an annual report. These all provide useful information.

Personal sources

Call one or two people on your networking list who may be acquainted with your target company. Find out the "inside scoop" from people who work for the company or have done business with the company.

Think about it

Answer each of the questions below in response to the following situation: Imagine some one calls to ask you to help them with an employment challenge.

What would the person say and how would he or she say it that would make it likely you would want to cooperate?

_____

_____

_____

_____

What would the person say and how would he or she say it that would likely make you less cooperative?

_____

_____

_____

_____

What type of common ground could a caller establish with you?

_____

_____

_____

What insights about networking have you learned from this exercise?

_____

_____

_____

_____

Three things you should do before you read the next chapter

1.   Set up a call record system on either 4x6 cards or in a data base management program. Provide a place to record relevant information about people on your networking lists.

2.   Outline an OGSM for two weeks of a networking campaign, using the example in the chapter as a model.

3.   Take an Internet test on your lifestyle choices.

      http://www.msnbc.com/modules/quizzes/lifex.asp This test helps you judge the impact of your lifestyle choices on your longevity. As you answer each question, you see the impact that lifestyle choice has on your projected length of life. Topics include blood pressure; health history; lifestyle choices such as smoking, exercise, diet and vitamin intake; driving habits; marital status; stress; social support; and sense of humor. This site is helpful because it shows you how many years you can add to your life if you make the right choices.

Your OGSM plan (first week)

Objectives	Goals	Strategy	Measurement

Your OGSM plan (second week)

Objectives	Goals	Strategy	Measurement

Chapter Five

Writing effective networking materials

*If you want to run the show someday and run it well, you had better
learn to think, write and speak in that order—clearly, forcefully,
concisely and to the point.*
Ed Artzt

The medium is the message.
Marshall McLuhan

Chapter Objectives

✔ **Writing effective networking materials**

✔ **Job search business cards**

✔ **Networking letters and e-mail**

✔ **Thank you letters**

✔ **Job announcement e-mail**

Many employers view what you write as the best indication of your
business ability. So it is important that you take extra care to make
your written materials as impressive as possible. Your goal is to present
yourself in a favorable light. When you project a positive image of
yourself, people you contact will see you as deserving of their time and
will want to share their experience, expertise and contacts with you.
This chapter discusses how to plan your written communications for
your networking campaign, including job search business cards,
networking letters, thank you letters, and job announcements.

In Chapter 7, you will find further useful advice on writing materials
related to your broader job search objectives. These include how to
write a letter of application, a variety of resumes, a thank you letter
subsequent to a job interview, and a letter of confirmation after
accepting a position.

Job search business card

A good investment is a job search business card which you design as a mini resume. Keep a supply with you at all times and hand them out freely. Business cards are a valuable aid because they often remain in a rolodex or business card file and thus are not as easily lost as a resume or letter.

The front side should include your name, address, tele #, and, if applicable, e-mail, voice-mail, fax, and website addresses. On the reverse side summarize your work experience, skills, and key attributes. See Figure 5-1.

Figure 5-1: Job search business card

(side 1)

Joseph Benjamen
7436 Plantation Road
Lafayette, NJ 07845

973-489-xxxx (tele/voice mail)
973-489-xxxx (fax)
jbenjamen@tapnet.com (e-mail)

(side 2)

Four years experience as first line supervisor
Excellent knowledge of automobile industry
Bachelor's degree in management, UCLA (1995)
Reliable, high energy manager with proven
leadership abilities
Outstanding record of cost savings and on-schedule
production runs

Exercise:
Develop a job search business card similar to the model above.

```
┌─────────────────────────────────────────┐
│                                           │
│                 Front                     │
│                                           │
│                                           │
│                                           │
│                                           │
│                                           │
│                                           │
└─────────────────────────────────────────┘
```

```
┌─────────────────────────────────────────┐
│                                           │
│                 Back                      │
│                                           │
│                                           │
│                                           │
│                                           │
│                                           │
│                                           │
└─────────────────────────────────────────┘
```

Networking letters and e-mails

Networking letters and e-mails introduce you to prospective contacts. Show you value your reader's time by keeping these messages to one page or one screen. A networking letter should open with a positive statement about the contact to whom you are writing, followed by your request for assistance. In the middle paragraphs, summarize your credentials and specify what networking materials you are enclosing. When your readers finish this section, they should have a clear understanding of your reasons for writing. In closing, express your thanks for the expected help and indicate when you will call and what you want to discuss. If you currently hold a position, indicate that you want your message kept confidential.

Figure 5-2:
Networking letter

Dear Ms. Cragen:

As the insurance agent my parents have done business with for the past ten years, I know you are a respected member of the Muncie business community. I am writing to you to see if you can provide some assistance to me. I'd be interested in getting your ideas about how I might find opportunities for work in the Muncie area.

After working for the last two years at MicroTech in Indianapolis, I am exploring opportunities at other firms. I have an excellent record as a marketing research associate and want to continue to work in the marketing field, including sales, advertising, or research.

For your information, I have included a resume and an information card that succinctly summarize my work experience, accomplishments, and goals for the future. As I am currently employed, confidentiality is essential.

I would greatly appreciate any information you can provide. I'll be calling you next Tuesday morning to get your perspective on the local business climate as well as any advice you have to offer on marketing-related job opportunities in Muncie. Should you want to call me, my home number is 765-987-5544. Thank you!

Sincerely,

June Mason

Exercise:
Using the above letter as a model, write a networking letter to a person on your list.

Your networking letter

Open with a positive statement about the contact to whom you are writing, followed by your request for assistance.

_____

_____

_____

_____

Summarize your credentials.

_____

_____

_____

_____

Tell the reader what networking materials you are enclosing.

_____

_____

_____

_____

Express thanks for the expected help; indicate when you will call and what you want to discuss

_____

_____

_____

_____

Networking e-mails:

Also consider using e-mail as a networking tool. E-mail has emerged as a mainstream medium of communication, with the number of users growing by 25% a year. You may substitute an e-mail for any networking communication. When you do, keep in mind the following guidelines.

Consider the advantages and disadvantages of e-mail

E-mail has several advantages—and two significant disadvantages—over traditional paper-based communication:

✔ **It is more convenient**, letting you send and read messages 24 hours a day, 7 days a week, 365 days a year, across time zones.

✔ **It is faster**, with turnaround time often measured in minutes versus the hours and days typical of paper based communication. A down side to this advantage is while you usually have some time in which to retrieve a letter before it leaves your building, few current e-mail systems allow you to retrieve sent messages for further revisions.

✔ **It is more efficient** and cheaper than letters (derisively called "snail mail") or phone calls. It allows receivers to respond at a time and place of their own choosing.

✔ **It is less predictable**. What you see on your screen may not be what your readers will see on theirs, because your contact's mail system might translate your message into an unattractive format on his or her screen.

✔ **It is less impressive.** You can more easily communicate high regard in paper communication through use of heavy bond paper, high quality laser printing, and a variety of document design techniques such as boldface and italics, impressive fonts, and selected type sizes. In an e-mail, you have relatively few document design techniques at your disposal. Overall, an e-mail has far less "curb appeal" than a letter.

✔ **Write an interesting subject line**. As your subject line is the first thing your contact will see, make it informative and compelling. Phrase it so its first words tell your contact what you want him or her to do in response to it.

✔ **Begin with a Dear (Dr., Rev., Mr., Ms., Mrs.).** While networking is a casual medium, it is safest to use a formal introduction until your contact tells you it is appropriate to use his or her first name. Avoid outdated forms of reference such as "To whom it may concern," "Dear sirs," or "Gentlemen."

✔ **Start with a friendly greeting**, such as "Good Morning," "Good Afternoon," or "Greetings." This will help you establish a personal touch in what many consider an impersonal medium.

✔ **Limit your message to three concise paragraphs**. This will allow your entire message to fit on a single screen and indicate you respect your reader's time.

✔ **Use a simple closing, such as "Thanks" or "Best regards."** Avoid abbreviations such as THX (thanks), which may be unclear or seem flippant to the reader. Also avoid formal closings, such as "Sincerely yours," "Cordially," and "Respectfully," which are more characteristic of formal written communication.

✔ **Design your document so it can be read on different terminals.** Not all e-mail systems are created equal. The message you see on your screen might look quite different on your receiver's terminal. To make sure your message looks good on all terminals, follow these guidelines:

> **Press "Enter" at the point at which you want each line to end** rather than using the wraparound feature. Different terminals may wrap at different places, producing an irregularly shaped message which may frustrate or confuse readers.

> **Limit line length to 60-80 characters.** On some terminals your message may not wrap and some characters on each line may be cut off.

Avoid features such as boldface and italics because the receiver's terminal may not be able to reproduce these effects.

Some guidelines for effective use of e-mail

✔ **Proofread carefully.** Proofread e-mail at least twice before you send it—once sent it usually cannot be retrieved. Check content as well as mechanics. Be sure that your message is written so it can be easily understood—and also so that nothing in it can be misunderstood. Use your spell checker only after you have completed proofreading—as a final check—and not as the only check on the accuracy of your e-mail.

✔ **Write networking e-mails on your own time and own computer**. Be careful about using e-mail at your workplace for networking purposes. Companies have the right to search e-mail mailboxes as they pay for the system and may resent the idea that you are using their system on company time to help find employment elsewhere.

✔ **Check your e-mail 2-3 times a day**. Your contact may immediately respond by e-mail to your request for a meeting and expect you to respond with equally fast timing.

✔ **Use both upper and lower case letters**. This format meets your readers' expectation for courteous text. All caps look like shouting. All lower case letters suggest the writer did not think enough of the reader to exert the effort to hit the capital key. You may use all caps for subject lines and other headings.

A networking e-mail follows a similar organizational pattern to the networking letter with certain restrictions. First, it should be exceptionally concise, designed to fit on a single computer screen. Second, it needs an informative and compelling heading, so it gets positive attention in the reader's directory. Two examples follow.

Figure 5-3:
Networking e-mail for a person with little
work experience

To: Ben Weinberg

Subj: SHARING EXPERTISE ON A CAREER AS A TRAINING PROFESSIONAL

Good morning! Elliot Shriberg suggested I e-mail you because of your success as Director of Training at Sun Electronics. I'd like to learn about the reasons for your success and the steps you recommend I take to begin a career in this field. I will finish my Human Resources degree in May from Iowa State University and want to learn as much as I can from outstanding real world experts about the challenges and opportunities for corporate trainers.

I would be honored if you would be my guest for breakfast or lunch next week to discuss these issues. With your permission, I will fax you a copy of my resume today and will call Thursday morning to follow up.

With warmest regards,

Chris Dixon

Figure 5-4:
Networking e-mail for a manager
with extensive past work experience

To: RAYMOND MARTIN, Vice President of Human Resources
        Exxon Corporation

Subj: A REQUEST FOR ASSISTANCE FROM PHIL EUSTIS

Dear Ray:

Greetings from Phoenix! I am Phil Eustis and you might recall we shared a pleasant
lunch at last year's national meeting of the American Society of Training and Development in Los Angeles. I kept your business card and am now writing to ask you for a
simple favor. If you are called, as I have been in the past, by recruiters looking for a
manager of training and development, I would be grateful if you would mention my
availability and let them know where I can be reached.

I am not asking for a reference, simply assistance in getting my name out. An attachment
containing my resume will give you an idea of my education and experience. If you
would like to communicate further about this matter, please call me at 1-602-555-xxxx.

I appreciate your help. Please let me know if there is any way I can return the favor.

Thanks,

Phil Eustis

Your networking e-mail

To:

Subj:

Open with a positive
statement about the
contact to whom you
are writing, followed
by your request for
assistance. Summarize
your credentials.

_____

_____

_____

_____

_____

_____

Tell the reader what
networking materials
you are enclosing.

_____

_____

_____

_____

_____

_____

Express thanks for the
expected help;
indicate when you will
call and what you want
to discuss.

_____

_____

_____

_____

_____

_____

Thank you letters

In the thank you letter, you have two objectives:

> ⇒ **to express your gratitude**

and

> ⇒ **to promote your business objective, whether to help advance a job application, request additional leads, or strengthen a positive working relationship.**

When writing thank you letters, provide specific information that reinforces your purpose. In writing to a contact, express your appreciation for the help you received and summarize what you perceive as the mutual benefits of your partnership—such as agreeing to help the contact in the future if the need should occur.

Consider sending a thank you e-mail if, and only if, you know your contact exceptionally well, or if you have previously written a thank you letter for past contributions and are e-mailing to express appreciation for new help.

Figure 5-6:
Networking thank you letter

Dear Ms. Yonushewski:

Thank you for taking time from your busy schedule to talk to me about opportunities in fashion merchandising. During our talk, I was delighted to see that you found your work to be so challenging and so highly rewarding. I am now more motivated than ever to pursue my goal of being a fashion merchandising manager.

You indicated that the typical career path for a fashion merchandiser in your company started on the department store floor, progressed to assistant buyer, buyer, and finally fashion merchandise manager. As I have had significant successful retail selling experience in a large department store and have kept current on fashion trends, I am confident I am well prepared to sell fashion merchandise. If you know of any companies that are currently hiring sales associates with my qualifications, please let me know and I will send my resume and business card to them immediately.

Again, I appreciate the information you gave me about the field of fashion merchandising. I was especially inspired by your passion for it. If there is ever anything I can do to repay your kindness, please let me know.

Warmest regards,

Nancy Viviano

P. S. I have enclosed a disc with web addresses for the sites of three designers the fashion press has identified as trend setters in evening wear design. I believe you will find these as thought-provoking as I did.

Exercise:
Write a thank you letter or e-mail to a networking contact

Thank contact

_____

_____

_____

_____

Provide additional
information and/or
ask for additional
help

_____

_____

_____

_____

Express appreciation
for the help. Offer to
return the favor

_____

_____

_____

_____

P. S. with information
relevant to contact's
interests

_____

_____

_____

_____

Job announcement letter:

After you have secured a job, write a letter or e-mail to every contact announcing your job and title, thanking them for their valuable assistance, and offering to help them when the need arises. If you do not send a thank you letter, you may create the impression you had no more interest in your contacts than helping you find your next job.

Figure 5-7:
Example of a job announcement
letter or   e-mail

Dear Ms. Yonushewski:

I have great news to share!

Starting May 12, I will be the new Assistant Acquisitions Manager at SouthWestern Publishing Company. This job will enable me to use my interpersonal and writing skills to help bring outstanding textbooks to college and high school students.

I want you to know how much I appreciated your help as I searched for an appropriate position. If there is anything I can do to return your kindness, please let me know. My new work number is 513-530-xxxx.

With warmest regards,

Chester Louganis

Exercise:
Write a networking job announcement e-mail.

Opening

 _____

 _____

 _____

 _____

Job
information

 _____

 _____

 _____

 _____

Statement of
appreciation

 _____

 _____

 _____

 _____

Keeping your network alive

Be sure to keep your network alive by viewing your networking
list as a resource that you will nurture through future communication. To create a "learning network" that will benefit a wide
range of contacts, look for ways of providing information,
insight, and help that meet the needs of those in your
networking circle.

Summary

Everything you write should be an outstanding reflection of your talents. Using the models highlighted in this chapter and adapting them to each networking situation will help you do just that.

Networking exercise

Assemble a portfolio of self promotion materials. You will select appropriate items from these materials to include in an interview kit each time you go to a networking or job interview. Your portfolio should include your business card resume; lead cards; 1 and 2 page resumes; certificates for awards that you have received; thank you letters for a job well done; copies of nonproprietary presentations you have made, including a disc containing PowerPoint slides you created; website addresses for webpages you have developed; photos of equipment on which you have worked; videos you have made; evidence of your ability to write well, such as letters, memos, reports, and proposals; and carefully selected A papers from school which demonstrate a skill, such as graphic design, survey research, spreadsheet or financial ratio analysis abilities.

Think about it

Marshall McLuhan said that "the medium is the message." That is, the way you send a message can have a dramatic influence on the way people react to that message. Using your experience as a guide, what does sending a message using each of the following media say about the relationship you have with and the regard for a receiver.

To send

  A letter vs. a fax

✔ **A letter vs. an e-mail**

✔ **An e-mail vs. a fax**

Three things you should do before you read the next chapter

1. **Go to a major business supply store such as Staples or Office Max and investigate different methods and costs of getting job search business cards printed**. Consider both programs which allow you to print cards directly from your computer's printer and having the store print the cards for you.

2. **Think carefully about what you can offer people who help you achieve your networking goals.** A good network is based on the principle of exchange. People will often help you because they believe they will receive something valuable in return. Write down your answers in the space below.

_____

_____

_____

_____

_____

_____

_____

_____

_____

3. **Go to** *http://collegegradjobs.miningco.com/mlibrary.htm* **on the Internet to find useful information on career planning and job hunting for new college graduates**. This site also contains links on adult and continuing education, as well as links to a variety of sites with information on different career fields.

Chapter Six

Preparing for telephone and face-to-face interviews

A single conversation across the table with a wise person is worth a month's study of books.
Chinese proverb

Start with where people are before you try to take them where you want to be.
Anonymous

Chapter objectives

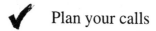 Plan your calls

✔ Make out a calling schedule

✔ Make the networking telephone call

✔ Manage the networking meeting

✔ Deal with objections

After you have prepared good written materials, you can begin the all-important oral communication phase of your networking campaign. The steps include planning, scheduling, and making your calls, preparing for meetings, and making a good impression face-to-face.

Plan your calls

1.   **Find out about the company**. It's dangerous to go on a blind date! You can use library and Internet research techniques to find out about companies. Ideally, you should know what the company sells, its level of annual sales, its position in its markets, how many people it employs, who and where its customers are, and the nature of its competition.

2. **Find out about the person you are going to call**, including the full name, its correct spelling and pronunciation, and the direct dial telephone number. Typically you can find out this type of information by calling the company switchboard. You can also find it in companies which are listed on stock exchanges by calling their investor relations department. Plan to use the contact's name during the interview to demonstrate your personal interest in the contact.

3. **Review your accomplishments lists**
    ⇒ List the talents and specialized skills you possess that are needed for the job
    ⇒ List the character traits which are important for the job
    ⇒ Make a list of questions to ask the contact
    ⇒ Anticipate what questions you expect to be asked and write out answers to them

4. **Think of ways of establishing credibility with the contact.**

Ask yourself the following questions:

How can I demonstrate common ground with this contact? Job experience? schools? geographic location? voluntary organizations?

What can I honestly offer the contact in return? How can I offer ideas or assistance in exchange for the help I will be receiving?

How can I position my comments so that they encourage my contact to meet my expectations for him or her? How can I position my initial questions so they will be easy for the contact to answer?

How can I demonstrate genuine interest in my contact? By asking my contacts to talk about their greatest successes on the job? By asking what brings them the greatest happiness on and off the job? By allowing my contact to have "center stage" and to talk without interruption?

Before you make calls, rehearse your personal pitch. Aim for the right balance of naturalness and conciseness. Consider including information about your past work experience, education, skills, expertise, personal qualities and accomplishments.

Review what you will say to introduce yourself, how you will communicate your purpose, how you will state your qualifications, what questions you will ask, and how you will answer the questions you are likely to be asked. Then mentally edit your responses to improve them.

Some have found it helpful to ask a colleague to play the part of the contact and then record and play back the conversation, so both can help improve the delivery and content of your networking message. See if you speak at an easy-to-understand rate, with a voice that is neither loud nor harsh. Make sure you sound friendly and approachable—like the kind of person your contact would like working with.

You may find you can communicate energy and enthusiasm more effectively by standing as you talk and by looking into a mirror from time to time to make sure you are smiling and upbeat during the entire conversation.

Motivating yourself to network on a daily basis

Calling someone you know for help is difficult enough. Calling someone who does not know you is even harder. Follow the steps below to motivate yourself so that your networking routine becomes a daily habit.

1. **Visualize the possibilities**. Remind yourself that each call holds out the possibility that it could lead to the best job of your life. Review how your talents and accomplishments are a platform for showing contacts how you could benefit their companies.

2. **Use positive reinforcement to help you stick to your calling schedule.** To motivate yourself, establish a reward system such as putting a quarter in your pocket for every call and a dollar for every call that leads to a productive face to face meeting. Don't stop calling until you have five dollars.

3. **Be organized and prepared**. Take time at the end of each day to go through your lead cards and determine who you will call the next day. Have your achievement lists in a permanent

place next to the telephone where you can easily retrieve them. You should be able to tell your contact about your strengths, the types of people you like to work with, and the kinds of challenges that motivate you.

4.   **Be concise**. Plan your calling script around your call objectives: to find out information that will help your job search, to set up face to face meetings with the most promising contacts, and to get referrals for other contacts.

5.   **Work without interruption**. The more you network, the more natural, relaxed, and efficient you will become at making networking calls.

6.   **Be persistent**. It may take 5-6 calls to get to an outstanding contact who can really help. Keep a positive outlook.

7.   **Put rejection into perspective.** Ask yourself "what's the worst possible thing that can happen?" *the contact will hang up? refuse to speak with me? treat me rudely?* or *ask me to call back?* None are life threatening and you always have the potential to succeed with future calls to new and better contacts.

Making the networking telephone call

You are now ready to make the networking phone call. This interview has four parts: the greeting, the biographical sketch, questions, and closing. Read the script from beginning to end and then do the following exercise.

Exercise:
Jot down ideas for your telephone script in the right hand column, using the model as a guide.

Model script	Your script
Opening: Good day! Mr. Ganger, this is John Clark.	Identify yourself
I am calling at the suggestion of Erika Smith, who worked with you previously in the Credit Department at General Electric.	Cite your reference plus the nature of the relationship
She and I served together in the Kentucky National Guard	Cite your relationship to reference
I am seeking career development information, and Erika thought you would be an excellent source of information on industry trends in the retail sales field, given your current position as General Manager of a K-Mart store. I would appreciate about ten minutes of your time.	State your objective
Biographical sketch: Let me first tell you a little about myself. I believe my experience, personality, and education are well suited to successfully working in retail sales. I have worked both full and part time at two major retail chains: Wal-Mart and J. C. Penney. My supervisors have consistently praised my promptness, courtesy, and perceptiveness in dealing with a variety of customer situations.	Write out your biographical sketch *Claim *Proof of claim
I completed my bachelor's degree in political science last year at Auburn University. I have also taken a variety of continuing education classes that have enhanced my customer service skills, including Personal Selling, Public Speaking, and Diversity. As you can see, I am well prepared to succeed in retail sales and eager to learn as much as I can about this field.	*Summary

Questions	Your questions
What are the main tasks and responsibilities of this position?	_____
	_____
What are the advantages of a career in retail sales? disadvantages?	_____
	_____
What are the standards for accountability?	_____
	_____
What opportunities are there for advancement? What trends will affect the future of retail sales management?	_____
	_____
	_____
What kinds of classes, activities, jobs, or experience would be most valuable for a person applying for this position?	_____
	_____
What kind of personal traits are important to success?	_____
	_____
Given the biographical sketch I presented, how well have I prepared for a career in retail sales?	_____
	_____
	_____
Who else do you know that it would be useful for me to contact?	_____

Closing

Write out your closing

Thank you for taking the time to speak with me. I have learned a great deal that I know will help me as I pursue my career goals. I will be sure to follow up on the leads that you have given me. With your permission, I will send you some resumes and business cards in case you want to call me or come into contact with someone who could help me further.

Express thanks

Commit to follow up on promises

Again, I appreciate your help. Please call me if there is any way I can return the favor.

Agree to help contact in future

Managing the face-to-face meeting

Networking by telephone is an effective initial networking step. Even more powerful is the networking meeting. Face-to-face networking is significantly more effective at generating successful job leads than is telephone networking. On the other hand, it is also far more time consuming—you can often make ten calls in the time it would take to complete one face-to-face networking meeting.

You should ask for networking meetings only with your most promising leads. These would include contacts who are most likely to know about jobs or be in a position to hire you—and with those contacts with whom face-to-face networking is the norm, such as local contacts you can make within your personal, social, and professional organization circles where you can have a networking discussion as part of your normal meeting activities.

The key to success in face to face meetings is to develop a meeting strategy. Key issues include when you will meet, how you should dress, meeting etiquette, and how you will communicate nonverbally and nonverbally.

Figure 6:1
Communicating the right image

Interviewers will make judgments about you based on all the information they perceive, including your appearance, verbal and nonverbal communication and correspondence. Importantly, you should manage your behavior so you project the following images of yourself, key personality criteria used by hiring authorities.

⇒ **serious about work, prepares well for tasks**
⇒ **confident, eager to do a good job**
⇒ **energetic and healthy**
⇒ **friendly, courteous, and personable**
⇒ **trustworthy, reliable, and unprejudiced**
⇒ **good oral, written, and interpersonal communication skills**
⇒ **goal-directed**

When you should meet

Request a time when your contact is less likely to have to meet other objectives, such as breakfast before work, a half-hour before lunch or quitting time, or dinner. In each case, the contact is less likely to feel pressure to end the meeting to attend other company meetings or appointments.

What you should wear

Interviewers will make judgments about you based on first impressions. So what you wear is important. Prior to the meeting, ask what appropriate dress will be so that your clothing will match your contact's. Typically, it is best to dress conservatively, with a classic understated look. Clothes should be clean, pressed, and wrinkle free. They should fit well, with pants breaking just above the shoe, and sleeves reaching the base of the hand. Shoes should be well polished. Wardrobe experts also suggest limiting the size and amount of jewelry and wearing only a modest amount of fragrance.

Before the meeting

⇒ **Confirm the details** of the meeting, including directions, date, time, and place.

⇒ **Prepare an interview kit** which includes business card resumes; 1 and 2 page resumes; lead cards; letters of commendation; award certificates; copies of nonproprietary presentations you have made, including PowerPoint; photos of equipment on which you have worked; videos you have made; addresses for websites you have developed; correspondence with the company or the interviewer; accomplishment lists; pens; and grooming supplies.

⇒ **Be on time**. Plan on being 10 minutes early and use the first 5 minutes of your time to check grooming for hair, clean nails, and neat arrangement of clothing. If your meeting is in an office building, locate and use the public bathroom in the lobby rather than ask the contact's secretary where the company bathroom is.

⇒ **Come with an agenda**. Especially if you asked for the meeting, an agenda will allow you to appear to be organized and prepared to spend the meeting time productively.

⇒ **Demonstrate executive presence:** Make a good first impression. And practice proper etiquette. It motivates people to look forward to speaking and working with you, and it enhances your reputation as a professional.

Here are some tips:

first impressions

✔ keep your shoulders back and stomach in: most recruiters prefer a candidate who looks physically fit

✔ walk at a moderate pace with a confident carriage

✔ smile with both face and eyes

✔ establish direct eye communication

business etiquette

✔ wait for interviewer to extend hand

✔ use a moderately firm handshake

✔ sit down only after being invited to do so

✔ sit up straight, with no slouching

✔ sit reasonably still, nod to indicate agreement and understanding, lean forward to indicate interest, and gesture with open hands. Avoid fidgeting of any kind

✔ practice good listening skills; speak only when you are sure you are not interrupting your contact

✔ show you are interested in the contact by asking questions that allow the contact to speak positively about his or her talents and accomplishments

✔ bring a pencil and pad; make careful notes of your discussion

✔ thank the interviewer for spending time with you.

Verbal communication:

Make it an objective to think before you speak. Keep your comments upbeat. Avoid contradicting an interviewer or making inflammatory or contradictory statements. Show you have a good—and tasteful—sense of humor. Indicate you respect your interviewer by sincerely complimenting his or her professionalism. And keep it positive, using words and phrases that communicate positive images of you. For example, it is preferable to say, "I have demonstrated a commitment to total customer satisfaction," than "I have a lot of experience dealing with customer complaints."

Figure 6-2: Use positive words and phrases

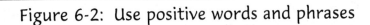

Use words and phrases that communicate positive images of you

> **team player:** *we, our, team, coordinated, take advice, work for consensus, learn from experience, mentor*

> **manager:** *plan, organize, schedule, motivate, follow through*

> **leader:** *goals, objectives, initiate, take charge, do whatever it takes*

Avoid words and phrases that communicate negatives images of you.

> These include *frustrated, incompetent, tired, trouble, no future, difficult boss, too much work, bored, problem.* There are no *problems*, there are only *opportunities for improvement!*

> Avoid the language of weakness ("I can't"), inflexibility ("I've always"), and wishful thinking ("If only I had").

> Use a positive vocabulary in preference to a negative one. For example, say you "improved the accuracy of the forecast" in place of "reduced errors in the forecast."

> Avoid weak phrases, such as "I *hope* to be successful in this position" or "I *think* I performed well in that role" or "I'm *sorry. I forgot* to mention that ..." These can undermine an image of leadership.

> Avoid talking about issues you find embarrassing, such as how and why you failed a class or were fired from a job. Don't bring them up—see if your contact does instead. Do not contradict or argue with the interviewer. Do not say any thing negative about past employers, teachers, or companies.

Leave when time is up:

Show you respect your contact's work responsibilities and other appointments.

Thank your contact for taking time to hold the meeting by using a 4-step praise statement

⇒   I appreciate the help you have given me ....

⇒   This information has contributed significantly to my . . .

⇒   If you think of additional useful information, I would be eager for you to share it with me.

⇒   Thank you for your support.

Figure 6-3:
Getting rid of "ums"

A famous shampoo ad reminds us that we "never have a second chance to make a first impression." So getting rids of verbal tics, such as "ums," is crucial to creating a positive impression. Fortunately, we typically use verbal tics in a consistent pattern.

To eliminate them, tape record yourself making a practice networking call. Each time you say "um," repeat that sentence, and you will find yourself about to say "um" at the exact same place. Keep practicing this exercise until you can anticipate and then work to replace each "um" with silence. Research also suggests that people say fewer "ums" when they gesture as they speak.

Networking meetings

Now that you know how to prepare for a face-to-face interview, let's look at an example of a networking meeting. Typically there are six steps:

√   greeting, identification of who referred you to the contact
√   small talk
√   objectives/ biographical information
√   fact finding and problem solving
√   resources/referrals
√   follow-up/request for additional help, such as a resume review

Example of face-to-face interview

Greeting: Begin with a positive greeting, mention the contact's name and identify who referred you to the contact.

Hello, Ms. Wilson. I'm Jennifer Dalton. Marilyn Maxwell spoke highly of you when we worked together on a Habitat for Humanity project and referred me to you because of your excellent knowledge of the human resources field.

Small talk: Ease into your objective with some pleasant small talk.

Contact: How is Marilyn?

She's very happy with her position at the University of Cincinnati.

Contact: Oh, that's interesting. When I last spoke to her, she was director of personnel at Tastemasters.

Yes, she moved to UC last year to direct the school's diversity program, an area in which I understand you and she share an interest.

Contact: Yes we do. I have developed our company's diversity training program and probably should compare notes with Marilyn's experience. Now, how can I help you?

Objective/biographical information: State your objective and concisely present your credentials.

Marilyn told me you have an excellent grasp of the likely issues that human resources managers will face in the future. I am currently pursuing work in the human resources field, and she recommended that I speak to you as a contact who could help me understand the field and its employment opportunities.

Contact: I see. Specifically how do you think I can help?

I have two questions for you: first, what areas of the human resources field are growing the fastest? And second, what companies do you know of that are expanding and might be looking for human resources help?

Contact: Good questions. Before I answer, why don't you tell me something about yourself?

I have five years work experience, all related to human resources. In my most recent position at Scott Paper, I also worked closely with our company's legal staff to develop a class on writing to avoid legal liability, especially with regard to health, safety, and environmental issues. And I played an important role in arranging counseling for employees who were released as a result of downsizing.

I also have an excellent education, having earned a bachelor's degree in management from Tulane University in 1994. At this point I am looking for a position that builds on my program development, interpersonal communication, and public speaking skills.

Fact-finding and problem-solving. Ask and answer questions concisely; allow the contact to speak freely and without interruption.

Contact: Why did you leave the Scott Paper position?

Actually, when Scott had its second major downsizing, as the junior member of the HR department, my position was eliminated. I left Scott on very good terms. My supervisor, Violet Ross, would, I am sure, give me an outstanding recommendation.

Contact: Given your past work experience, I would suggest that you highlight your strength in the legal realm, one of greatest areas of current business concern—especially with the increases in job related civil rights suits, such as sex, race, and age discrimination.

Resources/referrals: Ask for further contacts who could help you achieve your goals

Who do you know that could help me understand the opportunities in the legal area?

Contact: Mark Scott of Frost and Taft is our company's outside legal expert. He could probably give you a list of names to call. We have been very impressed by the depth of his knowledge about a variety of legal issues of concern to our industry.

I will follow up with Mr. Scott immediately. Can you think of any companies that are seeking the type of HR expertise that I offer?

Contact: Lockwood Engines. After it downsized, it was hit by a number of lawsuits alleging unlawful termination. Their new Vice President of Human Resources is Maria Delgado. You might call her and see if you can sell her on the idea that using your legal expertise will help them deal with these issues.

That's a terrific idea. Is there anything I should know going into this interview about the company or Ms. Delgado?

Contact: Maria is highly pressed for time. I suggest you offer to take her out to breakfast. You should do research to show you know a lot about the company's products, financial history, stock performance, and legal challenges. Mark might be able to give you some insight into how you could show Lockwood your value in helping protect the company from lawsuits.

Can you think of any other companies?

Contact: Not off the top of my head.

Follow-up: Tell the contact how you will follow up on the meeting.

Would you mind if I leave you copies of my resume so you will have a permanent record of my address as well as my fax, e-mail, and phone numbers? Then if you think of anyone or anything else, you could easily transmit the information to me.

Contact: Please do.

Thank you. And please feel free to pass my resume on to anyone you believe could help me. I really want to thank you for your time. I have learned so much. If I can return the favor in any way, please call me.

I will leave you copies of my resume and I will be sending a thank you letter today. I will immediately call Mr. Scott and Ms. Delgado as you suggested. I appreciate everything you've done. I hope we get to speak again soon.

Thank you telephone call

Once you have called or had a meeting with someone to whom you were referred, you should thank the person who gave you the referral. If you know your networking contact well, a telephone call may be the best way to say thank you. A call has a significant advantage over a letter, fax, or e-mail. It is interactive. You remind your contact of your goals, may be able to establish stronger rapport, and may receive additional useful information.

Here is an example of a thank you telephone call.

Hello Joan. This is Sue Bartlett. I'm calling to thank you for referring me to Janet Mason. She provided me with invaluable help in understanding the career opportunities available in public relations. Janet also gave me a lead on a job at Kahn's for which I am interviewing next week. I would never gotten this opportunity without your help. If I can ever help you in any way, just let me know.

Leaving an answering machine message

Many times when you call you will be connected to an answering machine. Be sure you have a clear plan for messages you will be leaving on answering machines. Provide only the most relevant information: name, number, reason for calling, and return call availability. Make sure your voice generates friendliness and enthusiasm.

⇒ **State your first and last name slowly and clearly**: This is Michael Collins.

⇒ **State your phone number clearly**: My number is 973-530-xxxx.

⇒ **Say why you are calling**: As we agreed last week when you spoke at our campus AMA meeting, I am calling to discuss career opportunities in the field of graphic design.

⇒ **Say when you will be available to receive a return message**: I will be in my office until 5:00 today, May 6, and from 8:30-12:00 tomorrow.

⇒ **Repeat your phone number slowly**: Again, my number is 973-530-xxxx. I look forward to hearing from you.

Creating a voice mail message

Review your voice mail to make sure it communicates a professional image of yourself. Update it frequently. Deliver it in clear, easy-to-understand language, at a relatively slow rate, and with a positive, cheerful tone. Do not have a cute message, background music, or a long introductory comment before the beep.

⇒ **Start with an upbeat greeting**: *You have reached the voice mail of Joan Hollins on Thursday, June 22. I am not available to take your message.*

⇒ **Indicate how the other person can or will get a response:** *Your call is important to me. Please leave your name and number, and I will be back to you within 24 hours.*

⇒ **Close on a positive note**: *Thank you—and make it a great day!*

Dealing with objections

Not all networking contacts are initially cooperative. Some may raise objections. When this happens, it is important for you to keep the conversation going. Here are responses to some of the most common objections.

We are not hiring	*I am not asking for a job, only a moment of your time so I can gain the value of your experience and expertise in this field. *I understand. I would like you to get to know me in case you do hear of an opening or would share other information which will help me in my job search. I will certainly be willing to return the favor.
I am busy	*This will only take minutes. I am willing to meet with you outside of normal work hours.
Send me your resume	*Let me fax it to you and then I will call back later today. *Let me tell you what is on it and I'll fax a copy to you later today.

Summary:

Successfully using oral communication skills, both on the telephone and face to face, is key to networking success—it is where your contacts make their most lasting and important judgments about you. By practicing the skills in this chapter, you will make a positive impression in both arenas.

Networking exercise

Attend at least two local meetings of an association whose members work in career fields you are considering. Examples include the Human Resources Association, the American Management Association, the American Marketing Association, and the National Association of Management Accountants. You should be able to find a list of organizations and their officers from your local Chamber of Commerce or public library. Call an officer and ask if he or she would serve as your host at the next meeting and introduce you to other members. (You may be expected to pay for your meal.)

Once at the meeting, engage some of the people you meet in conversation about what they find most rewarding and most challenging about their jobs; about their career paths; about what they see as the best preparation for a person interested in a career similar to theirs. Ask for business cards, a ready source of networking contacts who have met you, know your field of interest, and know other professionals in that field.

Later, call your most promising contacts and ask if you could have a meeting with them, or even better, shadow them through one or two hours of their or a subordinate's daily work, as a way of experiencing the reality of their day to day work life. If you get the opportunity to shadow, volunteer to help while there to reinforce an image of competence, cooperation, and gratitude.

Think about it

The way you send a message can have a dramatic impact on the impression you make on a contact. As you did in Chapter 5, using your own experience as a guide, describe the different impacts on a contact of making the following decisions.

⇒   **A voice mail message vs. a completed telephone call**

⇒   **A telephone call vs. a face to face meeting**

⇒   **A letter vs. a telephone call**

⇒   **An e-mail vs. a voice mail message**

⇒   **A telephone call interrupted by call waiting vs. an uninterrupted telephone call**

⇒   **A telephone call to a person using a speaker phone vs. a telephone call to a person who is speaking directly into the headset.**

Three things you should do before you read the next chapter

1.   Read the following guides to business etiquette on the Internet.

Concise guides to executive etiquette

   http://www.ultranet.com/~phillips/

   http://www.eticon.com/busetiq.htm

E-mail etiquette

   http://onbusiness.net/articles_html/
   MarjorieBrody,CSP_111.html

Internet etiquette

   http://www.albion.com/netiquette/

2.   Imagine you are going to meet with one of your contacts. Write out a script for a face-to-face interview using the script in this chapter as a model.

3.   Think of questions you can raise in an interview that will show you can make an immediate positive impact on the interviewer's business. For example, as you converse with a hiring authority, you might ask "Has your staff used the Lexis Nexus database to explore the legal issues involved in an unlawful termination lawsuit?" or "Do you like the special effects PowerPoint 7.0 adds to presentations?" List similar questions you could raise that could reveal a special talent that would distinguish you from competing candidates.

Chapter Seven:

Writing the resume and other job interview materials

Whenever one of my people has an idea,
I ask him to lay it out in writing.
Lee Iacocca

Chapter objectives

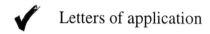

✔ Letters of application

✔ Resumes

✔ Thank you letters

✔ Letters of confirmation

✔ Letters written after being rejected for a job

✔ Letters written to decline a offer

Once your networking contacts have helped you find a job opportunity, you will typically need to support your candidacy with a letter of application, a resume, and a thank you letter. How well you compose these messages can often be the difference between being offered a position or being rejected.

Letters of application

In writing a letter of application, your key task is to prove that you deserve an interview because you are the best qualified applicant for the position. To make this point, you must demonstrate that your education, experience, and personal qualities precisely meet the criteria for the position. Before you write this letter, make a two-columned list. In the right-hand column, list the key criteria for the position. In the left-hand column, write down specific personal details which correspond to each of the criteria. Then use this information in a persuasive application letter.

In the first paragraph, name your contact and state your purpose in applying for a specific job. In the middle paragraphs a) indicate how and why your credentials are an outstanding match for the position; b) why you want to work for this particular company; and c) why you have the personal qualities it takes to succeed in this position. End by asking for the interview, indicating when you will be available to interview and to begin work. Be positive and upbeat throughout. To create a positive first impression, laser print your letter on quality white or cream paper and send it unfolded in a 9 x 12 envelope.

Sample letter of application 1

64 Oak Terrace
Racine Wisconsin 53402
414-999-xxxx
zaunbrecher76@hotmail.com

DIAMOND VIDEO STUDIOS
235 South Sixth Street
Chicago, IL 60614

Attn: **Renee Harris**
Director, Human Resources

April 27, 1999.

Dear Ms. Harris:

Your purpose in writing—if you have been referred for the position, mention it immediately

On the advice of Ms. Amy Perrin, a fellow human resources manager, I am writing to you concerning the video operations summer internships at Diamond Video Studios for the coming year. I met Ms. Perrin at last week's AST&D meeting and, after we reviewed my credentials, she gave me your name and number and encouraged me to list her as a reference.

What you have to offer—lead with your strongest credential

I am applying for this internship because my experience, education and personal qualities are an excellent fit for a video operations internship at Diamond Video Studios. I am eager to share my portfolio with you. It contains videos I have produced, including Give Peace a Chance, which won recognition at the National History Fair in 1996; a video on the life of John Lennon which I prepared for a college electronic communications class assignment; and videos and soundtracks I have developed for a variety of family celebrations.

My portfolio also demonstrates my writing skills, including well written papers I have prepared for a variety of classes at the University of Texas, where I am a junior majoring in mass media.

Why you want to work for this company

I am excited about working for Diamond because I want to be part of one of Chicago's fastest growing companies. Should you interview me, you will find that I am upbeat, reliable, creative, and cooperative—and eager to help any way I can throughout the term of the internship. I am confident I can both learn from your experts and also contribute to your success.

Next steps

I would welcome the opportunity to discuss this challenging opportunity more fully. I will finish my final exams on May 3 and will return to my home in Racine on May 4. I can interview and be available to work after then. The enclosed resume summarizes my qualifications. I will call you next week to discuss the potential for a personal interview.

Sincerely,

Otto Zaunbrecher

Your letter of application

Your purpose in writing—if you have been referred for the position, mention it immediately

_____

_____

_____

_____

What you have to offer—lead
with your strongest credential

_____

_____

_____

_____

Why you want to work
for this company

_____

_____

_____

_____

Next steps

_____

_____

_____

_____

You might also consider a less traditional approach to the cover
letter as illustrated below. In this letter you write the criteria for
the position in the left hand column of the body of the letter and
how you meet those criteria in the right hand column. This format
makes it easy for readers to see that you fulfill all the criteria for
the job.

Sample letter of application 2

The Creative Factory
855 Roberts Run Road
Dallas, Texas 75217
Attn: Mr. Michael Costura
      President

745 York Road,
Hunt Valley, Md. 20130
410-555-xxxx
CXA2@fusenet.com

15 April 1999.

Dear Mr. Costura:

I am writing to apply for the position of product analyst at The Creative Factory, a position for which Robert Craig of your Finance Department thought I was well qualified. He told me you were looking for a "entrepreneurially-minded, degreed, self-starter with previous experience in marketing and product development." I am well qualified, having relevant work experience and education to assure my success in this position. My resume is attached.

Success criteria	*My outstanding experience and education*
1. Marketing and product development experience	I am now a Product Development specialist at The Procter & Gamble Co. In this position, I worked closely with an outstanding team of product development and marketing specialists to improve the consumer acceptance of a noncarbonated beverage targeted to children. Our efforts resulted in a quadrupling of sales in three years.
2. Entrepreneurial self-starter	In college I started a highly successful tanning business, which generated $100,000 in sales for each of the two years I owned it.
3. Superior education	I received a degree in Chemical Engineering (1997) from Cornell University, graduating *cum laude*.

I believe my portfolio of an outstanding record of product development, marketing, and educational success will prove to be an effective platform from which to build a successful career at the Creative Factory, one of Dallas' most innovative speciality product manufacturers.

I look forward to the opportunity of discussing my employment with you in the near future. I will call you later this week with the goal of scheduling an interview for this position.

Exercise:
Write a letter of application for a job based on the model above.

Your letter

Purpose in writing,
mention referral
when appropriate

_____

_____

_____

_____

What you have to
offer, strongest
credential first

_____

_____

_____

_____

Why you want to
work for this company

_____

_____

_____

_____

_____

_____

_____

_____

Resumes

The resume is a persuasive summary of your qualifications for a particular job. It has one primary purpose— to win a job interview. No matter what your current standing, you should develop a resume now. If you are a student with several years to go before graduation, it may help you secure a valuable internship or summer job. And it will make you more conscious of what you should do in the next two or three years to make yourself an attractive candidate for a full time position. If you currently hold a job, having a well-organized, up-to-date resume will allow you to take advantage of unexpected opportunities within and outside of your current company.

To begin developing information for your resume, use the networking information you gathered. What skills, qualities, and achievements would describe the perfect candidate for a job you want? What special abilities does this person have? What would set a truly exceptional candidate apart from a merely good one?

Then focus your efforts on proving you match the profile of the ideal candidate. Include information from your past employment, volunteer opportunities, and education. Look at the lists you made in Chapter 3 and draw the best proof from each that matches each of the job criteria. Make readers see that if they hire you, they will get tangible benefits, such as cost savings, sales increases, improved security and safety, or reductions in employee turnover. This is the key to motivating a company to create a job for you—that you can help it achieve important goals. Your resume should also convince the employer that you possess the personal qualities it takes to be successful in the new position.

As you are targeting each job, you may have to modify your resume to meet the expectations of your reader. That is, you may change how you write your job objective, your summary, and even the evidence you select for describing your value in previous jobs to make sure it best meets the criteria the hiring authority has for the job.

Some information is required on all resumes: a) your name, home and college addresses, e-mail address, and phone number, immediately identifiable and at the top of the first page, b) a listing of all jobs held since beginning your career, in reverse chronological order, c) educational degrees including the highest degree received, also in reverse chronological order.

Jobs listed should include your title, the name of the firm, the city and state of the firm, and the months and years employed. Jobs earlier in a career can be summarized, especially those held while a student in high school or college. Second part-time jobs may also be omitted. Also include professional certifications and other continuing education programs. When relevant, add sections on Honors, Activities, and References.

Review the criteria below for each of the sections of the resume. At times I will ask you to develop a section of your own resume by imitating some examples I have provided.

Name, address, e-mail, and phone number: Write out your first and last name, centered at the top of the page. If you are a student, list both campus and home addresses and phone numbers. Write down an e-mail address, a fax number, and a website address, if you have them. See Figure 7-1

Figure 7-1:
Name, address, and personal information

Steven H. Hall

1632 Middlebury Drive	Home: 801-984-xxxx
Salt Lake City, UT 84117	Work: 801-985-xxxx
E-mail: *hallshh@hotmail.net*	Fax: 801-985-xxxx
Website: *www.utah.ut.edu.hallshh*	Campus: 801-988-xxxx

Objective:

The job objective section is a place where you can tell employers how they will benefit from hiring you. Include an objective whenever you are changing fields or are attempting to persuade a company to create a position for you. While some books on resume writing indicate this section is optional, many employers expect a job objective section on the resume. They want to be sure that your job objective is compatible with the job for which you are applying. And they want candidates who have clear work and career goals. As a result, I recommend that you prepare a concise and compelling objective statement that is tailored to the job. Alternatively, if you have previous experience in the job for which you are applying, you can replace the Objective section with a title directly under your name such as

Phil Jackson
Basketball Coach

Writing good objectives is difficult. The objective statement should sound like the employer's description of the job and also focus on what you can do for the employer. Limit it to no more than three lines. (See Figure 7-2 for examples.)

Figure 7-2:
Objectives statements

The following objectives each make a strong case for the job applicant.

OBJECTIVE - *A commissioned sales position in an organization where an outstanding record of generating new accounts, exceeding sales goals, and generating long lasting customer loyalty would be needed*

OBJECTIVE - *A retail management position in the fashion industry where I can employ my outstanding knowledge of apparel trends*

OBJECTIVE - *Analyst position with an investment house that offers the opportunity to use my education and expertise in bond and commodities trading*

As a corollary, omit the job objective if you believe yours adds little value to your case. Avoid using vague phrasings, such as **OBJECTIVE -** *"New college graduate desires an entry-level position that offers challenges and opportunities for career progression."* Such language puts you at a disadvantage to applicants whose objectives indicate they have been planning their education and job experiences with a clear career goal in mind.

Exercise:
In the space below, write a job objective tailored to a job you desire. Begin with the job objective you composed in Chapter 2 and adapt it to sound like one of the model statements above.

Your job objective:

_____

_____

_____

_____

_____

_____

_____

_____

_____

_____

The Summary

The summary is an optional part of a resume. It is the place to include professional characteristics—*high energy, excellent creativity and a proven record for identifying opportunities for improvement, committed to a philosophy of continuous improvement, exceptional listening skills, persuasive writer and speaker*—which may be helpful in winning the interview. Sometimes this information can be incorporated into the Objectives statement. For some candidates, it works well as a stand-alone category.

Your summary should read as a natural transition from the objective. Gear every word to the position you are applying for, highlighting qualities you have discovered are most important for the job. The qualities you stress may change with companies. For example, you might stress expertise in applying to a Fortune 500 company—and congeniality and outstanding broad experience in a resume targeted to a small organization. Write it concisely, in four lines or less. See Figure 7-3 for examples of summary statements.

Figure 7-3:
Summary statements

Motivated, creative and versatile bank executive with two years experience in property evaluation and construction lending. Especially skilled at building long-term lending relationships with commercial developers and home builders. Excellent negotiation and collaborative problem-solving skills. Team player.

Three years experience as a development officer with a track record of producing outstanding results for a major private university. Committed to developing new sources of endowment funding to support private school education. Energetic self-starter with excellent listening, speaking, and interpersonal skills.

Exercise:
Write a summary that captures key personal qualities that support your ability to do a particular job effectively.

Your Summary

_____

_____

_____

_____

_____

_____

_____

_____

_____

_____

Work experience:

If you have at least a year's work experience after you received your degree, you typically place Work Experience as the first major category of information on your resume. List jobs in reverse chronological order. Include your job title, the company for which you worked, and the cities and states where they are located. Focus on the most recent and/or relevant jobs. Limit detail on the jobs early in your career. Include both months and years of employment. Do not leave out any dates. Many recruiters see these as "red flags" indicating a candidate was laid off or fired. An exception is your high school and college student years, when working part time for short periods is viewed as normal.

Skills and accomplishments:

When writing on-the-job accomplishments, be specific. Use numbers to show impact and to communicate you can think numerically. Include, when appropriate, praise from managers, customers, suppliers, and direct reports. Wherever possible, prove that you have the desired qualifications through clear strong statements of accomplishments, rather than a statement of potentials, talents, or responsibilities. Indicate results of work done and quantify these accomplishments.

Figure 7-4:
Work experience, skills and accomplishments

Human resources administrator ADP, Lee, Va   *1/99 - present*

Initiated and directed complete automation of the Human Resources Department, resulting in time and cost savings of over 25%.

Maintained an open door policy for all associates. As a result, the number of grievances filed has fallen by 90%.

Assistant vice president   Junior Achievement Orem, UT   *5/96 - 12/98*

Coordinated Junior Achievement Leadership Conference. Planned and organized a highly successful conference designed to train thirty-five volunteer leaders. Promoted three times in two years.

For every skill, accomplishment, or job described, use a powerful word which accurately describes your achievements. Begin each sentence with the most active impressive verb that accurately describes your achievements. Limit lists to five bullet points.

Figure 7-5:
Accomplishment statements

Trained employees	Saved money	Enhanced reliability
Improved safety	Upgraded security	Planned meetings
Motivated colleagues	Analyzed data	Simplified procedures
Expanded markets	Improved collections	Saved time

Exercise:
List your jobs, titles, and dates in reverse chronological order. Use action words and specific data in developing appropriate lists of impressive contributions you have made to organizations.

Jobs _____

_____

_____

_____

Dates _____

_____

_____

_____

Skills _____

_____

_____

_____

Accomplishments _____

_____

_____

_____

Education:

Education will typically be your first major category if you have just earned or are about to earn a degree. List educational institutions in reverse chronological order, degrees or licenses first, followed by certificates and advanced training. List all colleges you have attended. Include study abroad and any certificates you may have received as part of that program. Set degrees apart visually so they are easily seen. If you paid for a significant percentage of your education through scholarships, loans, and work, indicate it here. Highlight foreign language and computer proficiencies. For scannable resumes, discussed later in this chapter, list courses that contain key words related to the field in which you are interested.

Figure 7-6:
Education

Indiana University, Bloomington, IN (BS, *cum laude*, Information Systems, 1998)

Financed 100% of education through scholarships, loans, and earnings.

Proficient in SALSA, Access, Excel, Powerpoint, QBASIC, Visual Basic, Visual Analyst, Java, SPSS, Macromedia, Web page development, and Internet research.

Activities:

Employers pay special attention to activities when evaluating new college graduates. They view them as key indicators of an applicant's leadership potential. Include leadership roles and titles, committees and subcommittees of organized student activities such as student government or dormitory councils. Also consider including intramural sports and activities requiring musical or artistic talents.

Civic and community leadership:

If you have been in the workforce for several years, substitute civic and community leadership for activities. Include those roles or accomplishments that are best related to the job target and indicate that you acquired relevant job skills. For example, a bank teller who is applying to be a financial investment counselor would be wise to write that she was treasurer for her neighborhood association and had invested its funds wisely.

Figure 7-7:
Civic or community leadership

World Wildlife Federation, *Volunteer fund raiser*   *9/94-10/94*

Proven fund raising talents: raised $1900 in 21 days canvassing for environmental and conservation issues. Won recognition as top fund raiser.

Awards:

Include recent awards: these indicate that your talents were recognized by others, a form of objective proof. Examples include "Employee of the Month award," "President's Club for Outstanding Sales Achievement, " "Norman Jones Scholarship for Distinguished Entrepreneurship paper," or "Elected to Delta Sigma Pi business fraternity in recognition of academic achievement."

Professional affiliations:

Tell what organizations you belong to, especially those related to the position for which you are applying. For example, if you are looking for a job as a technical writer, indicate you belong to a medical writer's association and have attended some of its conventions. *(Tip: If you do not belong to the association that is most related to your job, join it. It's a great place to make contacts who know the business and the people who are hiring.)*

Personal interests:

Include especially when it is necessary for you to convey skills and qualities not listed earlier or to create common ground with the interviewer. You might include a talent such as photography which might useful in a number of jobs. Or you might report that you enjoy attending symphonies and plays, an indication of cultural sophistication, an important quality for some positions, such as business executive, consultant or financial planner.

References:

List 3 to 6 references on a separate, final page of your resume. If the recruiter is interested in you, he or she will be able to call directly and not ask you for them. In addition, it can improve the impressiveness of your credentials if the recruiter knows and respects a reference you have listed. References can include former employers, community leaders, teachers, fellow workers, and supervisors. To get the best references, ask for them immediately after finishing a class or project, or when a job ends. Give the recommender guidelines for what accomplishments, skills, and personal qualities you want covered and for what purposes you plan to use the letter. Be sure to give the recommender at least a week to compose the letter. Include no more than six references.

Other qualities of excellent resumes

Visual appeal

Think of the resume as an advertisement that is so inviting to read that the hiring authority will select it from a stack of correspondence and read it first. To gain curb appeal follow these graphic design principles: Have at least a 3/4 inch border. Prefer bulleted lists to paragraphs. Use a laser printer so your resume will look typeset. Use a standard font such as Times or Helvetica in 10 or 12 point size. Use high quality paper that is absolutely clean with no white out, smudges, or staples. Insert a line of white space between sections to give a clean uncluttered look. Consider using a resume formatting template such as those provided on most recent word processing programs.

Consistency

Choose a pattern of spacing, an order of information presentation or a format of highlighting and follow it throughout. For example, you might put the names of all organizations in boldface and underline the name of each job title. Place dates in parallel to one another to facilitate easy scanning of employment history.

Appropriate length

Prepare both one and two page resumes—the first for networking and first interviews with companies, the second for when you have a subsequent meeting with a contact or an employer. Limit lists to five bullet points, paragraphs to six lines. To conserve space, space better used to describe your accomplishments, limit academic degree descriptions to one line.

Avoid writing a 1 1/4 or 1 1/2 page resume. Be sure to fill the page on a one page resume. Leaving a lot of white space may suggest you have said everything there is to know about you. When you present one or two full pages, you suggest you have carefully edited your resume to include only the most pertinent information.

Perfect accuracy

You must have total factual accuracy including correct spelling, grammar, syntax, and punctuation—and no typographical errors.

Figure 7-8:
What not to put on a resume

The words "Resume" or "Vita" at the top of the resume
Fluffy rambling "objective" statements
Salary information or reasons for leaving jobs
Full addresses and zip codes of former employers
Personal statistics or a photograph of yourself
Religious or political affiliation
Dangerous interests such as drag racing or skydiving

Figure 7-9: Example of a one page resume

Michelle C. Myers

875 Queensgate Rd., Apt. 604
Roanoke, Virginia 24014

tele: (540) 680-xxxx
e-mail: mc.myers@fuse.com

OBJECTIVE   A retail management position with a strong emphasis on outstanding customer service, cross-selling skills, and effective inventory control

SUMMARY   Motivated, creative and versatile retail manager with four years experience in upscale retail sales. Especially skilled at building long-term relationships with large account clientele. Outstanding ability to manage inventory effectively. Superior record of training sales representatives in the art of cross-selling.

WORK EXPERIENCE

<u>Coles Department Store,</u>   Roanoke, VA   5/96 - present
Manager, Housewares Department
*Promoted from assistant manager to manager after six months
*Created Roanoke's first on-line gift registry system, a significant success in increasing Houseware's gift revenue, especially with corporate accounts
*Instituted an automated inventory plan that was key to increasing product turnover by 25%
*Trained over 50 part time sales representatives how to cross-sell products to increase average dollar total per sale
*Received bonuses for exceeding my departmental sales goals by 10-20%

<u>University of Virginia,</u> Charlottesville, VA   9/95 - 5/96
Resident Assistant, Walker Hall
*Managed dormitory wing housing 19 freshman residents
*Coordinated and programmed wing activities
*Enforced rules and resolved conflicts among residents
*Proposed, developed, and led a successful Resident Assistant morale program
*Oversaw Residence Assistance Office during duty hours

Student Assistant, Office of Multicultural Affairs   9/93 - 5/96
*Participated on a team that developed and scheduled multicultural programming
*Helped students find employment and scholarship opportunities
*Trained new student assistants

EDUCATION   <u>University of Virginia</u>, (BSBA in Management & BA in Spanish, 1996)
* Financed 100% of educational expenses through work, scholarships, and loans
* Learned effective time management, listening, and business writing skills
* Became proficient in presentation, database management, and spreadsheet software
* Read, write, and speak Spanish fluently

HONORS   University of Virginia Gold Key Award for Service
Mitchell Scaggs Leadership Award

ACTIVITIES   President, Black Student Union, 1996-97
*Membership increased 20% during my term
Reading tutor for children in local literacy program
Enjoy reading, aerobics, theater, and recreational softball

Figure 7-10: Example of a one page resume for a college student

3899 Victory Parkway   Phone 502-xxx-xxxx
Louisville, KY 40214   Fax 502-xxx-xxxx

Martin X. Cunningham

Objectives	**A summer internship in a Louisville accounting firm**
Summary	**Hard working, cooperative, and detail-oriented professional with excellent knowledge of accounting principles and practices**

Education   **University of Louisville (BSBA in Accounting, May 2000)**
- Admitted with distinction; recipient of 4-year trustee scholarship for academic distinction
- GPA: 3.63; Dean's List every semester; 4.00 in accounting major
- Financed education through scholarships, loans, and part time work
- Experience with spreadsheet, graphic, presentation, and data base management software

Work Experience   **1997-present   Gallatin YMCA   Louisville, KY**
Customer Service Representative
- Provide access to members and security for their possessions
- Assist members in using equipment and facility in a professional, prompt, and courteous manner
- Maintain superior cleanliness of the locker rooms
- Assist manager in closing the facility
- Employee of the Month, 10-97 and 01-99

1996-1997, Summers Kelly Tire and Battery   Springfield, OH
Delivery Driver
- Demonstrated excellent customer relations skills
- Promoted after one month with a 10% raise
- Identified as hardworking and personable

1995-1996   Butler County Road Dept   Eaton, OH
Road Maintenance Crew
- Part of team that helped maintain county roads
- Trained new employees on work procedures, safety techniques
- Supervised maintenance of tools, supplies, and vehicles
- Accomplished daily work priorities as established by director of roads

Extracurricular activities
- Accounting Society, 1997-present; Treasurer, 1998-99
- Enjoy the Arts Society, 1997-present
- Coached CYO basketball for two years, leading team to district championship, 1994-1996
- Intramural softball, football, and basketball, 1997-present

Figure 7-11: Example of a two page resume

GREGORY DI BATTISTA

16 Red Cloud Court
Kokomo, IN 39193
tele: (317) 756-xxxx

e-mail: gregdb@tapnet.com
web: http://christhosp~battista/index.html
fax: (317) 763-xxxx

OBJECTIVE   Director of Medical Education and Research in a major medical teaching center known for the quality and effectiveness of its residencies.

SUMMARY   Ten years experience as an associate director of medical education and research. Track record of producing outstanding results for a major private hospital. Committed to developing new sources of funding to support medical education. Energetic self-starter with excellent interpersonal communication skills.

HONORS   First physician assistant hired by Christ Hospital in Indianapolis
Certified in both medicine and surgery for state of Indiana

EXPERIENCE

Christ Hospital, Indianapolis, IN

Associate Director of Medical Education and Research   **1990 - present**

Residency responsibilities
*Ensure compliance with general medical education certification standards
*Originate resident employment and rotation contracts

Research responsibilities
*Oversee all research funded with hospital monies
*Summarize research findings for hospital's research council
*Review and help edit all hospital-originated research prior to submission for publication

Medical education achievements
*Acquired and maintained certification for hospital as a Category 1 provider, resulting in $17,500 in annual savings for hospital.
*Developed over 100 category 1 activities per year.
*Developed a system to identify and prioritize educational needs of medical staff
*Appointed to team of Ohio medical education site supervisors
*Initiated a cross-training program which improved nurse morale and retention

Communications achievements
*Edited a newsletter to highlight medical education opportunities.
*Helped develop a web page for Christ which allows on-line registration, saving an estimated $48,000 per year in registry costs.
*Trained medical researchers on how to do research on the Internet.

Grant writing achievements

*Successfully wrote grant to fund the establishment of a "Scoliosis Prevention Program," now implemented in all Marion County sixth grade classes.

*Obtained federal grant money to support resident research on a variety of topics, including improved suturing and alternatives to antibiotic treatment.

Christ Hospital, Indianapolis, IN

Administrative Director, Department of Surgery   **1988 - 1990**

*Coordinated all surgical residents and department functions.

*Maintained quality control of resident training program; assured that all met "Essential" and "General" requirements established by certifying agencies.

*Prepared surgical certification reports; represented hospital at site survey.

*Established a visiting expert program for the department.

Senior Surgical Assistant   **1984 - 1988**

*Supervised, trained, and scheduled 24 surgical assistants

*Helped train interns and students in surgical techniques

*Served as operating room first or second assistant for Chief of Surgery

*Assisted surgical residents with patient care responsibilities

Surgical Assistant   **1980 - 1984**

*Served as operating room first or second assistant

*Assisted with patient care responsibilities

United States Navy

Corpsman   **1976 - 1980**

*Trained as anesthesia corpsman and field medical technician.

*Administrative Corpsman, 1st Hospital Company, FMF

EDUCATION **Indiana University-Indianapolis** (MBA, 1998)
Christ Hospital, Indianapolis (RN, with honors, 1984)
Miami University-Hamilton (AA, Applied Science, with honors, 1982)
Ball State University (BA, American Studies, 1976)

COMPUTER SKILLS Windows 95, Microsoft Word, Works, Excel, PowerPoint 7.0, Authorware, Lotus Notes Learning Space, Internet research, Web page design

OTHER SKILLS Certified lifeguard, including first aid and CPR
Certified mediator in non-violent conflict management

ACTIVITIES Member of Physician Assistant Advisory Committee, Miami University-Hamilton
Kokomo Volunteer Rescue Squad
Cub Scout First Aid Instructor
Rotary Club

Scannable resumes

Scannable resumes are growing in importance as more and more companies are turning to technology to screen resumes. When defining job requirements, hiring authorities will select a group of key words that reflect the skills needed for that position. Then scanning equipment "reads" resumes and selects those for further review that pass the match test. As a result, these resumes have to be attractive to the scanner's eye, even if they are not to the human eye. Here are some hints for writing scannable resumes.

1. You may input as long a resume as you like because the computer does not tire or get bored when reading several pages. Your name should be at the top of every page.

2. Use only capitalization for highlighting. Using italics, underlining, or shaded areas may confuse the scanner.

3. Font size ideally should be 12; 10-14 is also within range. Stick to commonplace fonts such as Times, Helvetica, or Courier.

4. Resume pages must not be folded, nor should they contain staples.

5. Resumes should be printed off a laser printer, not reproduced on a photocopier.

Content suggestions for scannable resumes

Use key words and acronyms relevant to the position you are applying for. For example, a human resources specialist might include the following words: *salary and benefits administration; training and development; expertise in employment law; excellent recruiting and interviewing skills; labor union negotiations; compensation expertise; performance appraisal skills.*

Listing topics covered in relevant classes and using terminology contained in want ads for jobs in your field are good ways to fill out a key words requirement. Also list every computer program you have mastered and every language you can write or speak. If you are not sure if a company has scanning equipment, submit two resumes. Put post-it notes on each, one saying "visual resume," the other "scannable resume."

Figure 7-12: Example of a scannable resume

Michelle C. Myers
875 Queensgate Rd., Apt. 604
Roanoke, Virginia   24014
tele: (540) 680-xxxx
e-mail: mc.myers@fuse.net

OBJECTIVE
A retail management position with a strong emphasis on outstanding customer service, cross-selling skills, and effective inventory control

SUMMARY
Motivated, creative and versatile retail manager with four years experience in upscale retail sales. Especially skilled at building long-term relationships with large account clientele. Outstanding ability to manage inventory effectively. Superior record of staff training in cross-selling. Experience with credit approval, new account set-up, and collections. Diversity training experience.

WORK EXPERIENCE
Coles Department Store,   Roanoke, VA   5/96 - present
Manager, Housewares Department

-Promoted from assistant manager to manager after six months.
-Created Roanoke's first on-line gift registry system, a significant success in increasing Houseware's gift revenue, especially with corporate accounts
-Instituted an automated inventory plan that was key to increasing product turnover by 25%.
-Trained over 50 part time sales representatives how to cross-sell products to increase average dollar total per sale.
-Received bonuses for exceeding my departmental sales goals by 10-20%.

University of Virginia, Charlottesville, VA   9/95 - 5/96
Resident Assistant, Walker Hall
-Managed dormitory wing housing 19 freshman residents
-Coordinated and programmed wing activities
-Enforced rules and resolved conflicts among residents
-Proposed, developed, and led a successful Resident Assistant morale program
-Oversaw Residence Assistance Office during duty hours

Student Assistant, Office of Multicultural Affairs   9/93 - 5/96
-Participated on a team that developed and scheduled multicultural programming
-Helped students find employment and scholarship opportunities
-Trained new student assistants

Michelle C. Myers

EDUCATION
University of Virginia, (BSBA in Management & BA in Spanish, 1996)
Completed classes in Business and Technical Writing, Retail Management, Small Business Consulting, Teamwork, Total Quality Management, Organizational Communication, Interpersonal Skills, Public Relations, Electronic Media, and Business Strategy
-Financed 100% of educational expenses through work, scholarships, and loans
-Learned effective time management, listening, and business writing skills
-Became proficient in presentation, database management, and spreadsheet software, including MS Word; MS Works; Excel; PowerPoint, and Access
- Read, write, and speak Spanish fluently

HONORS
-University of Virginia Gold Key Award for Service
-Mitchell Scaggs Leadership Award

ACTIVITIES
-President, Black Student Union, 1996-97
Membership increased 20% during my term
-Reading tutor for children in local literacy program
-Enjoy reading, aerobics, theater, and recreational softball

Skill-based resumes

If you are a new college graduate with little job experience, have been out of the workforce, are pursuing a radically different career path than your job history would suggest, or if your job progression has been unimpressive, consider writing a skill-based resume, such as the one illustrated below. It highlights your qualifications for a position rather than the chronology of your jobs or your education. This arrangement may allow you to make clearer connections between your capabilities and accomplishments and your job objective than would a traditional chronological resume.

Figure 7-13: Example of a one-page skills resume

Elaine Quan Zhou

64 Cherry Grove Lane
Evanston, Illinois 60201

tele: (847) 654-xxxx
e-mail: eqzhou@hotmail.com

OBJECTIVE

To use my proven teaching ability and superior understanding of effective selling strategies to create and deliver comprehensive and compelling training programs for account representatives.

SUMMARY

Motivated, creative and award winning executive with outstanding experience in sales and education. Especially skilled at creating short and long term training programs. Polished public speaker.

HONORS

Million Dollar Club, Wadsworth Press, 1998, 1999
National Finalist, Toastmasters International Public Speaking Contest, 1996
Teacher of the Year Award, Chicago, IL, 1983.

BUSINESS EXPERIENCE

Consultant   1998 to present
Wadsworth Press, Belmont, CA

Training and Promotion

Plan and present regional seminars to large and small groups
Create successful product and technical proposals for large accounts
Write direct marketing and promotional materials

Territory Management

Develop new markets and build share with existing accounts
Design, organize, and execute product and territory marketing strategies

Sales

Have won major textbook contracts with Chicago Public School System
Exceeded sales goals by 50% in 1998 and 1999

TEACHING EXPERIENCE

Language Arts Teacher, Grades 5-12   1975-1998
Chicago Public Schools, Chicago, IL

Curriculum Development

Developed, organized, and implemented curriculum for middle school
Managed classroom through small group activities and individualized learning programs. Directed "writing as a process" program in grades 5-8.

Program Administration

Initiated, innovated, and executed immediate, short-range, and long-range instructional programs. Chaired and coordinated curriculum committee and English Department. Produced and directed school plays.

EDUCATION

Loyola University, (MBA, 1996)   GPA: 3.80
Bowling Green State University (MEd, 1983)   GPA: 4.00
Ball State University, (BS, 1975)   GPA: 3.48

CONTINUING EDUCATION

Collaborative Selling   Face-to-face Selling Skills
Presentation Skills   Managing Diversity

CIVIC ASSOCIATIONS

Toastmaster's International, Past President of Evanston chapter
American Society for Training and Development

ACTIVITIES

Golf, tennis, recreational softball, reading, and music

In short, a well-designed resume establishes you as a professional who is well organized, writes well, and knows the importance of presenting yourself well. As a further benefit, when you develop and revise your resume, you will find it to be an excellent device for clarifying your strengths and abilities in your own mind, good preparation for telephone and face-to-face interviews.

Thank you letter

In the thank you letter written after a job interview, you have two objectives: to express your gratitude and to promote your objective of getting the job. When writing thank you letters, provide specific information that reinforces your purpose. For example, in a follow-up to a job interview, point out a new fact about yourself that proves you have a quality the interviewer mentioned as crucial for the position.

Figure 7-14:
Example of a thank you letter after a job interview

Dear Mrs. Rogers:

Thank you for the time you took out of your busy schedule to interview me. During the interview you indicated you were looking for a director of nursing who could skillfully initiate a strong cost control program while maintaining a high level of esprit de corps among fellow workers.

I am such a person, having already achieved these twin goals while employed at Bethesda Hospital in San Diego. During my tenure there, I effectively reduced total compensation costs for both pharmaceutical and registry nursing staff while maintaining the highest level of retention and lowest level of turnover in the hospital. Part of my success is attributable to an effective cross-training program I initiated.

As we discussed, I am challenged by the opportunity to help you establish a "business mentality" in the nursing area to help contribute to General's fiscal viability while also assuring that the care you deliver meets the highest standards. I am confident that General Hospital will benefit from my leadership skills.

I will call on February 28 to discuss next steps, unless I hear from you sooner.

Sincerely,

Deborah Rogers

Exercise:
Write a thank you letter to a person who has interviewed you for a job.

Thank interviewer
Indicate you want
the job

_____

_____

_____

_____

Provide further evidence
of your ability to do the
job well

_____

_____

_____

_____

Indicate what will
happen next

_____

_____

_____

_____

Letters of confirmation:

Once you have secured a position, write a letter confirming your understanding of some of the details of the position. This will help make sure your and you company are "on the same page" regarding your and their expectations surrounding your new position.

Figure 7-15:
Letter of confirmation

International Thomson Publishing
5100 Madison Road
Cincinnati, OH 45227
    Attn: Ms. Kathleen Silvera
        Acquisitions Manager

May 24, 1999.

Dear Ms. Silvera:

Thank you so much for offering me the opportunity to work with you at ITP as an assistant acquisitions manager. I am excited about the challenges and rewards this position offers—and I am confident I will quickly become a productive and valued member of ITP's team.

My understanding of the terms of my contract are as follows:

    Report to ITP on June 1 at 8:30 a. m.
    Work a 40-hour week, with weekend and overtime, as needed
    Earn a salary of $30,000 annually
    Receive full medical, dental, and retirement benefits, as well as life insurance equal to twice my salary
    Travel, as required, both within the USA and internationally

Please let me know if my understanding is correct. I appreciate the opportunity to contribute to ITP's creative team and look forward to beginning work with you on June 1st.

Sincerely yours,

Elinor Smith-Jones

Exercise:
Write a letter of confirmation for your ideal job.

Say thank you and that you are excited about the job opportunity

_____

_____

_____

_____

List the details of your understanding of the job

_____

_____

_____

_____

Ask for confirmation. Say you are looking forward to starting work

_____

_____

_____

_____

When you are rejected for a position

If you are rejected, write a thank you letter as a polite follow up. Express your appreciation for having the opportunity to get to know more about the firm. Indicate you believe you could contribute to the company's goals and suggest that the company take a second look at you should openings arise in the future. This persistence and grace in the face of rejection says something positive about you to recruiters—and may lead to a reconsideration of your credentials.

Figure 7-16:
Example of a thank you letter after receiving a rejection.

Dear Mr. Bagley:

Thank you so much for interviewing me for the staff assistant's position at Arthur Andersen. I appreciated learning more about the importance of the staff assistant's role to Arthur Andersen's consultants. Due to your professionalism during the entire interview process, I now have a higher opinion than ever of your firm and am convinced I could make a valuable contribution as a staff assistant.

Please keep me in mind should you have another opening for this or a related position in the near future.

With warmest regards,

Charlene Frost

When you decide to decline a job offer

If you decide to decline a job offer, take the time to write a tactful letter that invites the possibility of future contact. Open positively, state your reasons for the rejection, state your rejection explicitly, and close on a gracious note expressing your appreciation for the job offer.

Figure 7-17:
Example of a note declining a job offer

Dear Mr. Roberts:

I truly enjoyed my interview last month at your headquarters in Seattle. I was impressed by the commitment your management team displayed to being the world's best software provider. Thank you so much for offering me the position of assistant brand manager in your marketing department.

During my job search I also interviewed for a brand management position at a leading consumer products company in Westchester County, New York. As my wife has just accepted a full scholarship in NYU's excellent MBA program, and we want to remain together until her graduation in two years, I have accepted the other job offer.

I appreciate the time you and your associates spent talking to me about the brand manager position and your company's exciting plans for the future. Thank you so much for all the kindness and consideration you showed me throughout the interview process.

With warmest regards,

Michael Posey

Summary

Good writing to support your job applications can improve your chances of getting a job. By following the guidelines and imitating the models described in this chapter, you can demonstrate your professionalism in all your employment correspondence.

Networking exercise

Prepare four versions of your resume. Choose from either a) 1 and 2 page chronological resumes in both formal and scannable formats, or b) 1 and 2 page skills resumes in both formal and scannable formats.

_____

_____

_____

_____

_____

_____

_____

_____

_____

_____

_____

_____

Think about it

Your company is looking for a trainer who will help prepare newly hired financial analysts for securities licensing tests. Determine the strengths and weaknesses of each of the following pieces of job correspondence. Write down your suggestions for improvement in the margins. Ask one of your networking contacts to do the same and compare your answers.

Cover letter: Which opening paragraph of a letter of application would most attract your positive attention?

Dear Mr. Thomas:

Would you agree that an experienced trainer with an outstanding knowledge of securities licensing requirements would be a valuable addition to Fidelity's human resources staff? If that trainer also had advanced degrees in business and education—and had won awards for public speaking excellence, would you be interested in hiring her? I am Erika Bahir, and as you can tell, I have excellent credentials for the training position Mason Houston, a financial advisor in Fidelity's Trust Department, told me is now available.

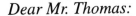

Dear Personnel Director:

My name is Erika Bahir. I have a bachelor's degree in Education and masters degrees in both educational administration and business management. I have excellent teaching experience and am familiar with the licensing requirements for securities analysts. I hope you would consider me for a training position. I understand from Houston Mason that one is available at your company.

_____

_____

_____

_____

Job Objective: Which of the following four job objectives would be most responsive to the specific nature of a training position at a securities firm?

An entry-level training position in a firm known for its commitment to continuing education.

A training position in which a degree in human resources and a knowledge of securities licensing requirements would be applicable

To use my knowledge of securities licensing requirements and my demonstrated teaching skills to create and deliver comprehensive and easy-to-follow training materials for prospective stock brokers

To contribute to a positive learning atmosphere in a successful and creative company where I could apply my knowledge of finance and human behavior

Education: Which description of education would be most attractive for this position?

Harvard University, Cambridge, MA (B.S.B.A., Human Resources Administration, 2000)
Graduated with a 3.2 average. Won Delta Sigma Pi Award in 1999.

Miami University, Oxford, OH (BA, Communication Arts, 1999; MBA, Finance, 2000)
Received outstanding graduate education in stocks, bonds, and other financial instruments.

- Made a number of highly praised presentations in my graduate business finance classes.
- Am proficient in word processing, spreadsheet, presentation, statistical analysis and data base management software. Expert in Web page design and Internet research.
- Financed 100% of college expenses through part time work, scholarships, and loans.

Indiana University-East, Richmond, IN (BSBA, Finance; BA, Spanish, summa cum laude, 1999)
- Graduated with 3.88 average. Dean's list every semester
- Awarded 4-year Honors Scholarship based on outstanding high school academic record
- Read, write, and speak Spanish fluently

_____

_____

_____

_____

_____

_____

_____

Three things you should do before reading the next chapter

1. **Use the following Internet resources to help you prepare job application correspondence.**

   http://www.rpi.edu/dept/llc/writecenter/web/text/resume.html covers topics such as self assessment and resume building.

   http://www.cce.edcc.edu/cce/jd120s/related.html which will link you to a variety of sites on cover letters and resumes as well as to further information on conducting the job search campaign.

   For additional information on effective job correspondence, go the Kaplan, Archeus, Jobsmart, and Wall Street Journal sites, referenced at the end of Chapter 1.

2. **Visit the following sites to get advice on how to prepare an on-line resume. You can submit your on-line resume directly to Internet job banks.**

   http://jobsmart.org/tools/resume/res-elec.htm

   http://wired-resumes.com for guidance on how to construct a multilevel on-line resume. This resource, for a small fee, submits your resume to on-line job banks.

3. **Write a cover letter for a job you want.**
   Go back to the exercises you completed at the end of chapters 2 and 3 in which you describe the ideal candidate for a job you desire. Write a want ad for that position. Then write a cover letter in which you effectively demonstrate that you meet the criteria for that position.

NOTES

Chapter Eight:

Preparing for the job interview

Many people are only one idea, one dream, or one person away from their miracle.
Bob Harrison

It is better to be prepared for an opportunity and not have one, than to have an opportunity and not be prepared.
Whitney Young

Chapter objectives:

 Effectively answering screening questions in job interviews

 Preparing for behavior based interview questions

You will know that your networking campaign has paid off when you receive multiple invitations for job interviews—and competing offers of employment—while others who limited their job searches to traditional avenues are still waiting for the phone to ring. Although a job interview can be intimidating, your networking efforts will have prepared you to succeed. You will communicate confidently because of your experience in initiating numerous telephone and face to face networking meetings. And you will show that you have an excellent understanding of a company and its competitive position because of the research you have done.

Getting ready for the job interview

Prepare for job interviews as you did for face to face networking meetings. Begin by reviewing your accomplishments lists and selecting 3-5 accomplishments, qualities and skills that prove you are the best person for this job. Also think about potential weaknesses, such as poor grades, gaps in employment, and lack of relevant experience an interviewer might identify and rehearse appropriate answers to them. And importantly, review what is vital to you in a job, so you can ask questions that will provide you with the information you need to determine whether or not you should accept the position if it is offered to you.

Keep in mind that when interviewers ask you tough questions, they are simply doing their jobs. Interviewers have two broad questions on their minds: *Can you do the job?* and *Would we like to work with you?* To help you prepare, call two or three of your most knowledgeable contacts. Ask them what questions they might pose if they were interviewing you for that position and what answers they would find most compelling. Also ask what issues you should raise and how they recommend you promote yourself for the position.

Before the interview, find out as much as you can about the interviewer, confirm the details of the meeting, and prepare an interview kit. Plan your transportation so you will reach the interview site ten minutes early—enough time to check your grooming and wardrobe, and still arrive in the interviewer's office five minutes early.

What to expect

Much like networking meetings, most job interviews have a common structure. They begin with small talk as the interviewer tries to put you at ease. The interviewer will then forecast the structure of the interview by indicating its purpose and the types of topics that will be covered. Toward the end of the interview, you will be expected to ask questions of the interviewer about the job and company. The interviewer will also expect you to listen respectfully while he or she tells you about the company and what it has to offer its employees.

Types of interviews

Most organizations do interviews in two stages. They first hold relatively brief screening interviews, interviews designed to identify the strongest candidates for the job. Successful candidates are then invited for longer interviews, which often include a variety of behavior-based questions, an interview approach that has gained increasingly wide acceptance in past twenty years.

Screening interview questions:

Job interviewers, like most networking contacts, are likely to ask you some basic questions about your preparation for work. The key to answering these seemingly simple questions is to understand the "question behind the question." Every question an interviewer asks has one purpose: to see if you are the right person for the job. For example, when recruiters ask you to "tell me about your education," you will not be responsive to their needs if you recite a long list of classes that you took, or make vague comments about how your education was a good preparation for the career path you have chosen.

Figure 8-1:
The questions behind the questions

The actual questions	The questions behind the questions
Tell me about your education	What have you learned that you can apply immediately to this position? Have you set consistent goals and had a plan for achieving them ?
Tell me about your work experience	What results did you achieve in other jobs that you can duplicate at our company? Did you work well with others? Are you responsible?
Tell me about yourself	Do you value qualities in yourself that we value in employees? Would we like to work with you? Will you fit into our culture?
What have you read recently?	Are you involved in a program of continuing education that is relevant to this job?
In what activities have you been involved?	Have others recognized your leadership abilities? Have organizations benefited because of your participation?

Rather your answer should focus on what would help interviewers sell you to their colleagues as the best person for the job. You might point out that you learned skills, such as data base management, report writing, or speaking fluent Spanish, which you could immediately use on the job. Additionally, you could prove that you planned your college courses, part time work, and activities around the single goal of a career in the field for which the interviewer's company is hiring. That answer would probably indicate that you were serious about the position and likely to make a long term commitment to it.

Also be wary of offering negative information about yourself. It will probably be used against you when hiring decisions are made. As an example, one recruiter was about to recommend that an interviewee have a further interview with his company when he asked a simple question, "Tell me about your weaknesses." Twenty minutes later, when the applicant finished her detailed analysis, he decided against a further interview!

You should also work on organizing your answers so they meet the interviewer's needs. Your answers should answer the question immediately; provide specific proof of your abilities, personal qualities, or positive impacts on organization; and end with a persuasive summary. Below are four frequently asked screening questions, strategies for answering them, and an example of an effective answer. Additional questions and space where you can write down answers to them is provided at the end of the chapter.

Question: __Tell me about your education.__

Strategy:
Begin by making a claim that your education taught you immediately applicable skills for the job. Then prove that claim with specifics. Only then should you describe the subjects you studied in school. Summarize by saying you are confident your education will help you make an immediate contribution to the company.

My education at The University of South Florida has provided a solid foundation for a position as financial consultant trainee at Fidelity Investments. For example, as part of my finance major I learned how to perceptively interpret data on income statements and balance sheets. This education will allow me to speak with the excellent finance vocabulary Fidelity clients expect from its consultants. I also learned to perform ratio analysis, so I can benchmark a company's performance against its competitors on a variety of standards.

In addition to my finance and accounting education, I took courses in marketing, business communications, and computer science to broaden my understanding of the field of business. I also completed a rigorous liberal arts core requirement. And I advanced my cultural education by attending a variety of movies, plays, and concerts that were offered on and off campus.

In short, I have the tools and background to be a financial consultant Fidelity will be proud to have represent it. I am committed to learning the job quickly so I can immediately contribute to the company's bottom line.

Question: **Tell me about your work experience.**

Strategy:
Relate your work experience directly to the job for which you are applying. Selectively show how past positions will help you with some aspect of the position.

I understand that in this position I will be coordinating the marketing activities for Chemed's large account development program. I have a solid background for this job. As a product manager who helped successfully market 25 industrial greases, I can help guide and implement sales and product development strategies to make sure each of Chemed's brands meets or exceeds the goals the company has set for them.

And I am confident I can effectively manage the people side of this position as well because I understand the jobs of the people who would report to me now hold. For example, as an applications engineer I helped customers get the best uses of our industrial products. As a sales rep I successfully built loyalty to our products with large and small market clients. And as a chemist I helped develop industrial lubricants. In short, my past experience has prepared me to successfully fulfill the position of marketing specialist at Chemed.

168

Question: Describe a weakness.

Strategy:
Identify a weakness you have already overcome and show how you turned it into a strength.

I learned the importance of time management my freshman year in college. After struggling with C's and D's in most of my classes, I went to the Learning Assistance Center for guidance. A counselor there told me I needed to improve my time management skills. I enrolled in the time management seminar the Center offers each month.

It was one of the most productive afternoons of my life. I learned how to write a to-do list, how to prioritize my projects, and probably most importantly, how to use a calendar to help me with long and short range planning. Instead of studying and writing papers at the last minute, I actually set goals for grades and plans for completing assignments well ahead of time, so I could review, revise, and perfect them. As a result, my grades soared and I learned a skill which has and will benefit me in all areas of my life.

Question: Why should I hire you?

Strategy:
Start by saying you are well qualified for the position. Then outline the reasons why you are well qualified. Next provide proof for that claim. Summarize your answer.

I have the right qualifications for a supervisory position with SuperValue Distributors. I have prior experience, excellent knowledge of the industry, and relevant course work. To pay for my college education, I worked first as a night laborer, and later as assistant supervisor for the second shift at Wayne Warehousing. I helped implement an inventory management plan that saved the company $25,000 a year. I also dealt directly with many large retail stores, communicating by phone, fax, e-mail, and in person with the purchasing agents from Sears, WalMart, and K-Mart.

I recently finished my marketing degree at Creighton University , where I learned how to conduct market and consumer research. In short, I bring work experience, industry knowledge, and an excellent education to successfully fill this position.

Preparing for behavior based interview questions

Once you complete the screening interview and are passed on to the next level of interviewing, you are likely to be asked numerous behavior based questions. Behavior based interviewing assumes that your past experience is the best predictor of your future behavior. Unlike screening questions, which are often open-ended in terms of what content is appropriate in an answer, behavior based questions ask for very specific information. For example, a typical behaviorally based series of questions is "Give me an example of a time when a co-worker criticized you in front of a co-worker? How did you respond? How did this event affect the way you communicated in the future?" If you do not give specific answers to each of these questions, the interviewer will ask you to provide them.

You will have to draw deeply from experiences you described in your accomplishments lists to answer behavior based questions effectively. To prepare for these interviews, take the following steps.

Determine from your networking contacts what the most important criteria are for the position and then search your past for examples that prove you successfully meet those criteria. This will help because in preparing for behavior-based interviews, interviewers prepare a list of questions intended to reveal if you have the competencies needed to be effective in the job.

Use your networking contacts and other research findings to uncover a target company's core values and recall experiences where your behavior has reflected those values.

Rehearse answers using real-life examples. It is very difficult to remember good examples during an interview. By practicing, you will be able to recall your past accomplishments with confidence.

Be detailed and specific. Many interviewers are taught to use the three part STAR process to evaluate an answer and to keep asking questions until the applicant addresses all three parts. These three parts are as follows:
1. **S**ituation or **T**ask
2. **A**ction
3. **R**esult or outcome.

For example, you might recount a time when communication within your work group had broken down. (Situation) To resolve the problem, you organized informal lunch meetings for people to discuss relevant issues. (Action) Morale then improved as did the lines of communication. (Result)

Using this three step STAR process is also a powerful way for you to frame your experiences and accomplishments for the interviewer.

*   Listen carefully to each question. If you are unsure, rephrase the question and ask for clarification. When you respond, be sure to recall your past accomplishments in detail.

*   Use the STAR pattern of organization in these interviews because that will help you prove to the interviewer that you have developed a complete answer.

Here's an example of a typical question, an appropriate strategy for answering it, and an answer which meets the interviewer's needs. Additional behavior-based questions and space where you can write down answers is provided at the end of the chapter.

Question: <u>**Tell me about a time when you demonstrated creativity and imagination on the job**</u>

Strategy:
Organize your answer so that your first sentence repeats a key word of the question. Then describe a situation in which you exhibited creativity to achieve an important goal for the organization.

One of the strengths I bring to this position is creative thinking. (Claim linked to question)

While working at Germania Park last summer, my crew was responsible both for disposing of garbage from the picnic area and with transporting empty bread racks back to the loading dock for restocking the next morning. (Situation)

The dumpster is located near the loading dock, so I suggested that we could place two empty bread racks on top of the bags of garbage each time we made a trip and get two jobs done at once. (Action)

As a result, we limited the overtime we often incurred previously when all the bread racks were moved to the dock at the end of the day. My supervisor liked the idea so much that it is still in use today. (Results)

Summary

Being able to effectively address questions and objections depends on being prepared for them. If you plan carefully for interviews, and practice answering tough questions such as those above and those covered in the end of chapter exercise, you will become increasingly adept at impressing interviewers with the excellence of your answers.

Networking activity

Go to the Alumni Office of a school you are attending or have attended and ask to see a list of alumni. Many colleges publish an alumni directory every five years. Identify two or three of the most successful alumni who work for a company you have targeted, are in a career field you are pursuing, or have attended a professional school to which you are interested in applying. Call to see if you could conduct a telephone or face-to-face interview. As with your association contact, ask if you could shadow them for an hour or two during their daily work.

Think about it

Take the following self assessment. Answer each question candidly and tabulate your total score.

1. When I meet someone I make out a rolodex card for them
    a. that same day
    b. within 24 hours
    c. within 48 hours
    d. within the week
    e. rarely

2. I follow up with new contacts by writing a note or leaving a voice mail or e-mail message.
    a. that same day
    b. within 24 hours
    c. within 48 hours
    d. within the week
    e. rarely

3. I am meticulous about the grammar and spelling in all of my correspondence, as well as the accuracy of names, titles, companies & addresses to everyone in my network.
    a. I personally check and ask another to check all my correspondence for accuracy.
    b. I check these issues 2-3 times before mailing.
    c. I check these issues once before mailing.
    d. I rely primarily on my computer's spell checker.
    e. I don't think it's realistic to expect 100% accuracy in these issues.

4. I have assembled a portfolio highlighting my abilities and accomplishments
    a. I can't think of what I would put into it
    b. I certainly intend to at some time in the near future
    c. I am beginning to make a collection of letters of recognition and other expressions of gratitude I have received.
    d. In addition to the above, I am assembling evidence of my ability to produce PowerPoint slide shows and videos.
    e. I have put together a comprehensive portfolio, including all of the above, as well as lists of machines, computers, and software which I can operate.

5. I have compiled a complete job history
   a. I have listed my previous paying jobs and my titles.
   b. I have listed all paying jobs, highlighting those job activities where I exercised the most responsibility.
   c. I have listed all previous jobs, titles, and tasks, including work I have done as a volunteer.
   d. In addition to the above, I have noted what I liked and disliked about each of my jobs.
   e. In addition to the above, I have listed the location and names of clients and suppliers and my contacts with them.

6. I am willing to help others when they ask me to do some thing that I believe is within my power and a reasonable use of my time.
   a. Rarely. I'm too busy.
   b. Occasionally, when and if I have the time.
   c. Sometimes, if I know the person very well.
   d. Consistently, if I know the person or if I was referred by a person I trust.
   e. Almost always, people know they can count on me to help.

Scoring

5 pts. 1A, 2A, 3A, 4E, 5E, 6E
4 pts. 1B, 2B, 3B, 4D, 5D, 6D
3 pts 1C, 2C, 3C, 4C, 5C, 6C
2 pts 1D, 2D, 3D, 4B, 5B, 6B
1 pt 1E, 2E, 3E, 4A, 5A, 6A

What your results mean

25-30 **A potential networking superstar!**
20-24 **Developing good networking habits**
15-19 **On the right track**
10-14 **You've a long way to go**
06-09 **It's time to jump start your efforts!**

Three things you should do when you have finished reading this chapter

1. Re-take these tests, which you completed at the end of chapter 1, to see how well you are now prepared for the job search:

   http://www.cweb.com/inventory/ How far have you come in your job readiness?

   http://cgi.pathfinder.com/cgi-bin/Money/goodnews.cgi How well are you now prepared for the work environment of the Twenty-first Century?

   Go to Kaplan website and take the Interview Challenge. You may have to take it more than once to get the job!

   http://www1.kaplan.com

2. Read more about behavior based interviewing at the following site

   http://www.brockport.edu/career/BEHAVE.htm

3. Read and answer each of the screening and behavior-based questions on the pages that follow. Use the suggested answers as a guide to organizing your own answers. As you network and interview for jobs, write down additional questions that you were asked. Develop thoughtful responses to each. Before you conduct subsequent interviews, review your list of questions and answers to refresh your memory.

Preparing for the job interview

Using the format suggested for the model answers in this chapter, answer each of the following screening and behavior based interview questions.

Screening questions

Why are you interested in the field of commission sales?

I have always had confidence in my sales abilities—from selling hundreds of boxes of wrapping paper, innumerable magazine subscriptions, and carloads of snack foods—all to help my participation in Boy Scouts, soccer camps, and band. **(Claim/evidence)**

I was successful because with each sales opportunity I set a challenging goal to win one of the top prizes offered for outstanding sales. **(Rationale)** I then mapped out a territory and faithfully called on each house. I continued to sell until I had reached my sales goal. **(Action)** As a result of my extra effort, I earned, among other things, a bicycle, soccer ball, and a Walkman CD player. **(Results)**

Your answer
(apply to your career field)

Claim:

_____

_____

_____

_____

_____

_____

_____

Rationale/Action:

_____

_____

_____

_____

_____

_____

_____

_____

Results:

_____

_____

_____

_____

_____

_____

_____

Tell me about your college education

I have received an outstanding education at College X, one that I tailored with an eye toward a career in sales. I majored in marketing and learned valuable skills including how to design and administer a survey, how to write a persuasive sales letter, and, of particular relevance to personal selling, how to anticipate and overcome customer objections. In fact, one of the most important lessons I learned was to practice "mental rehearsal," imagining that I was the intended audience and visualizing the likely response I would receive. (**Claims**)

For example, when I wanted to persuade my parents to let me have my car on campus for my sophomore year, I knew I had to overcome significant objections: that I would not use the car responsibly and that having a car would be a large expense and a distraction from my studies. To overcome these objections, I stressed that I would only use the car to travel to and from my job and to drive between home from school, that I would give up the car if my average fell below a 3.0, and that I would pay for all my car expenses out of my wages from my off-campus job. (**Action**)

They let me have the car, and I kept my promises. That one simple step —mental rehearsal—has really helped me develop an ability to look at situations through the eyes of the customer—a critical ability for any sales representative. (**Results/Learning**)

Tell me about your college education

Claims:

_____

_____

_____

_____

_____

_____

_____

Action:

_____

_____

_____

_____

_____

_____

_____

Results/Learning:

_____

_____

_____

_____

_____

_____

_____

_____

Tell me about activities outside of work that you enjoy.

As a Girl Scout Troop leader I demonstrated important managerial skills. **(Claim)** For example, I planned, organized, and scheduled weekly meetings; motivated girls to actively participate; and kept outstanding records, something that allowed me to successfully train my successor, when my daughter moved into a troop of older girls. I also encouraged the girls to become meeting leaders by having them meet in teams to plan and carry out awards ceremonies and campfire gatherings. **(Proof)**

And I taught the girls the importance of public service—as a group we gave hundreds of hours in service to homeless shelters, nursing homes and the Red Cross. **(Claim/proof)**

I also rewarded the girls with fun activities such as trips to Boston, Atlanta, and Orlando. My girls and I proved exceptionally talented fund raisers—and I learned to communicate and bargain effectively with travel agents and tour guides.

Additionally, I have learned the importance of working together when snorkeling, an activity I enjoy with my family. **(Claim)** For safety, we snorkel in twos or threes, pointing out beautiful fish and rock formations to one another, as well as possible dangers, such as string rays—all through the use of nonverbal communication. **(Proof)** Snorkeling has really made me appreciate the value of working with others to achieve common goals, a talent I will bring to your work environment. **(Significance)**

Claim

_____

_____

_____

_____

_____

_____

Proof

_____

_____

_____

_____

_____

_____

_____

Estimate of significance

_____

_____

_____

_____

_____

_____

_____

Use a similar logic to answer each of the following questions.

Describe the most rewarding experience of your life

Claim

_____

_____

_____

_____

_____

_____

Proof

_____

_____

_____

_____

_____

_____

_____

Estimate of significance

_____

_____

_____

_____

_____

_____

_____

Describe a strength you bring to an employer.

Claim

_____

_____

_____

_____

_____

_____

Proof

_____

_____

_____

_____

_____

_____

_____

_____

Estimate of significance

_____

_____

_____

_____

_____

_____

_____

_____

Describe a shortcoming. Thinking of the future, in what areas could you benefit from additional training?

Claim

_____

_____

_____

_____

_____

_____

Proof

_____

_____

_____

_____

_____

_____

_____

Estimate of significance

_____

_____

_____

_____

_____

_____

_____

_____

Other screening interview questions for which you should be prepared

Questions about your employment

Tell me about each of the jobs you have held starting with the most recent.
Describe your duties and responsibilities.
What did you like about the jobs?
What didn't you like about the jobs?

Questions about your education.

Why did you choose your college? (Hint: list solid criteria)
What subjects did you prefer? (Hint: those relevant to job you want)
What subjects did you dislike? (Hint: those where professor allowed little interaction)
What kinds of specialized training did you receive?
Did you receive any special recognition?
What extra-curricular activities did you participate in? any leadership roles?

Prepare answers to the following behavior based questions

Behavior based questions

Tell me about a situation in which you were able to motivate others to help a group achieve its goals.

I have used my knowledge of child psychology to help motivate children in a summer camp achieve both educational and behavioral goals. I have discovered that highly energetic children typically need outlets for their energy and also desire positive recognition. **(Claim)**

So, if I saw a child begin to engage in disruptive behavior, I would ask him or her to take the lead in picking up toys, getting athletic equipment, and helping younger children learn new activities. In this way I helped channel their energy into productive outlets, and I made sure I praised them when they helped out. **(Situation/ Action)**

As a result, the head counselor consistently praised my leadership abilities and even asked me to share my insights with the other counselors about how to motivate children through positive reinforcement. **(Result)**

Claim

_____

_____

_____

_____

_____

_____

_____

Situation/Action

_____

_____

_____

_____

_____

_____

_____

Result

_____

_____

_____

_____

_____

_____

_____

Tell me about a time when you had to "bend the rules" to achieve a goal.

I believe it is important to demonstrate integrity in any job, because integrity is the basis for trust and productive long-term relationships with customers, suppliers, and fellow employees. **(Claim)**

Once, at a retail outlet where I was working, a customer asked for a refund on a formal gown she had bought three weeks before. Our store policy was no returns on any formal dress after seven days, primarily because so many high school students were buying dresses for a prom and then returning them immediately after the dance. **(Situation)**

I knew this woman to be a frequent and good customer and told her what our policy was and its reasons—and that I would ask my manager if we could "bend the rule" because her situation was not one the policy was intended to address. **(Action)**

The manager approved the refund and thanked me helping the store retain an excellent customer, one who maintained her loyalty to our store. **(Results)**

Claim:

_____

_____

_____

_____

_____

_____

_____

Situation:

_____

_____

_____

_____

_____

_____

Action:

_____

_____

_____

_____

_____

_____

Results:

_____

_____

_____

_____

_____

_____

Describe a time when you were recognized for your ability to solve a problem.

Once I suggested a way to significantly reduce the amount of time needed to maintain sand traps while I was working as a groundskeeper at Terwilliger's Run Golf Course. (**Claim**)

I noticed that we were spending a disproportionate amount of time making the sand traps look good. We spent three hours each day raking each of 63 sand traps, and we also needed to re-edge the traps twice a year. Re-edging requires five workers to make a new edge on the bunker by digging up the area where sand had gone over the old edge and onto the grass. The average time to re-edge one bunker was two and one half hours. And after only one week, the bunker was no longer clean, with sand finding its way over the edge. (**Situation**)

I analyzed how we maintained bunkers and determined that the main cause of the problem was that we were driving the Sand Pro through the bunker and then hand raking the sand to the edge.

I suggested we first hand rake the edges and the finish the main part of the sand trap with the Sand Pro. (**Action**)

This method kept the sand away from the edges, thus keeping the edge of the ground showing. By using this technique we only have to re-edge the bunkers once every two to three years, a significant improvement in both the appearance of the bunkers and with a significance decrease in the hours needed to maintain the bunkers. (**Result**)

Claim

_____

_____

_____

_____

_____

Situation

_____

_____

_____

_____

_____

_____

Action

_____

_____

_____

_____

_____

_____

_____

_____

Result

_____

_____

_____

_____

_____

_____

_____

Please talk about a time when you had to work with a diverse group of people.

During a recent mission trip to Matamoros, Mexico, I learned that one must, as Stephen Covey says, "seek to understand before one seeks to be understood." **(Claim)**

I had come to Matamoros to help renovate a small church. Though I had learned classroom Spanish, it was of little use in this situation. At first, though I listened intently, I could only understand a few words of each sentence addressed to me.

I began using small phrases asking people to repeat what they said or to say it in different terms. For example, a man named Paco asked me to paint, but his words came too fast and I was unsure where and what I was to paint. I picked up a paint brush to let Paco know I understood I was to paint, but then I had to ask what and where he wanted me to. This time I understood what was said and to be sure, I repeated what Paco had said and pointed to what was to be painted. **(Situation/Action)**

It was necessary to use this technique of listening to all that was asked before responding throughout the trip. I learned that understanding must come before you respond and have applied this to all that I do. Understanding first has allowed me to learn faster and respond quicker both in school and at work. **(Result)**

Claim

_____

_____

_____

_____

_____

_____

_____

Situation

_____

_____

_____

_____

_____

_____

Action

_____

_____

_____

_____

_____

_____

_____

Result

_____

_____

_____

_____

_____

_____

_____

Other behavior based questions you should be prepared to answer:

Tell me about a time when you demonstrated resourcefulness and follow-through.

Claim

_____

_____

_____

_____

Situation

_____

_____

_____

Action

_____

_____

_____

Result

_____

_____

_____

_____

Describe a situation to me in which you demonstrated leadership.

Claim

_____

_____

_____

_____

Situation

_____

_____

_____

_____

Action

_____

_____

_____

_____

Result

_____

_____

_____

_____

Tell me about a time when it was important for you to use a key communication skill. (You should be able to describe situations in which either alone and together you used your skills in reading, listening, writing, public speaking, or one-on-one communication to achieve an organizational goal.)

Claim

_____

_____

_____

_____

Situation

_____

_____

_____

_____

Action

_____

_____

_____

_____

Result

_____

_____

_____

_____

Other behavior based questions you should be prepared to answer:

Describe a situation in which you used both logic and intuition to solve a problem or discover an opportunity to help an organization meet its goals.

Tell me about a time when you used something you learned in school or in a continuing education program to complete work on the job.

Tell me how you manage stress.

Give me an example of a time when you were criticized in public. How did you respond?

Describe your system for keeping track of multiple projects.

Tell me about a time when you failed to meet a deadline. What did you fail to do? What were the repercussions? What did you learn?

Describe an unpopular decision that you enforced. What was the result?

APPENDIX I:

Additional internet resources to help you find available positions

America's Employers	www.americasemployers.com/
America's Job Bank	www.ajb.dni.us/
Career Magazine	careermag.com/careermag/
CareerMosaic	www.careermosaic.com
Career Web	www.cweb.com/
College Grad Job Hunter	www.collegegrad.com
E*Span	www.joboptions.com/e
IntellitMatch	www.intellimatch.com
JobDirect	www.jobdirect.com
JobNet	www.westga.edu/'Ecoop/
Jobtrak	www.jobtrak.com
JobWeb	www.jobseb.org
Nation Job Online	www.nationjob.com/
100 Hot Job Sites	www2.100hot.com/jobs/

Appendix II:
Job search readiness inventory

Take the job search readiness inventory to assess how effectively you are implementing the guidelines of this workbook. Commit yourself to working on each area for which you record a "No" answer.

Job search readiness inventory

1. I am looking for positions at all sizes of companies, realizing that small businesses generate the vast majority of new jobs.

2. I have used **Thomas Register**, **The Encyclopedia of Associations** and **Directories in Print** as key networking resources.

3. I am devoting 5-15 hours a week to the job search process.

4. I am pursuing networking to gain increased control over my employment destiny.

5. I have lists of all the product and process knowledge I have acquired in my for-pay and voluntary positions.

6. I have determined how this knowledge could help clients of my previous business and their competitors.

7. I have analyzed what is most satisfying to me about a job experience and determined what types of jobs best meet my needs in that area.

8. I have realistically analyzed what is most important to me about the location of my job, including its impact on my family,

9. I have written out very clear, specific primary and secondary job objectives.

10. I have taken the time to make detailed lists of examples which prove that my efforts have benefited every organization for which I have worked.

11. I have made detailed lists of examples which show that I possess the personal qualities associated with successful employees.

12. I have inventoried my specialized skills, including licenses, foreign languages, ability to use scientific equipment and software programs, technical writing skills, public speaking, interpersonal skill training, and statistical analysis techniques.

13. I have reserved time weekly for reflection and meditation.

14. I have had a professional evaluate my business wardrobe.

15. I have made effective use of web resources in my job search efforts.

16. I have attended job and career fairs in my area.

17. I have access to lists of school alumni.

18. I am involved in a religious organization.

19. I am involved in a group sport.

20. I take advantage of opportunities for public speaking.

21. I have gotten to know my neighbors well.

22. I have had my business correspondence professionally evaluated.

23. I have made and maintain a list of former friends, co-workers, clients, and suppliers.

24. I have found someone who helps me with job coaching.

25. I have developed outstanding listening skills.

26. I continually work on my business etiquette skills.

27. I have worked on my telephone skills.

28. I have compiled an exhaustive list of professional colleagues.

29. I have compiled an exhaustive list of relatives.

30. I have compiled an exhaustive list of teachers and guidance counselors.

31. I have compiled an exhaustive list of church and social club members.

32. I have compiled an exhaustive list of members of professional and political organizations.

33. I have compiled an exhaustive list of members of professional and political organizations.

34. I have set up an effective "lead card" system on which to keep notes on networking calls and meetings.

35. I know the appropriate career path for the positions I am seeking.

36. I know the qualities an ideal candidate would possess for the positions I am seeking.

37. I have invested time in exploring all avenues of job search success including state employment agencies, newspaper ads, internet sites, and businesses I have specifically targeted.

38. I have set up good networking records.

39. I have prepared a "business card" resume.

40. I have set up "model" networking and job applications letters on my word processor which I can tailor to each networking and employment opportunity.

41. I have prepared a variety of resumes, including traditional, scannable, and skills based resumes.

42. I have developed an electronically based resume for use on the Internet.

43. I have set up "model" thank you letters on my word processor.

44. Before I make a networking call, I first find out about the person I am going to call and the company for which he or she works.

45. I have prepared and practiced a biographical sketch which I can use in both telephone and face-to-face interviews.

46. I have prepared an interview kit.

47. I have had an expert evaluate my executive presence, including my posture, carriage, eye communication, and nonverbal communication

48. I have worked to establish a positive vocabulary and a positive attitude toward my past jobs and supervisors

49. I have developed an appropriate list of questions to ask potential employers.

50. I have checked my voice mail message to make sure it is upbeat and positive.

51. I have prepared and practiced persuasive answers to tough questions about my education, activities, and employment.

52. I have prepared and practiced answers to a variety of behavior-based questions.

Appendix III:
If you lose a job

Objectives

Be prepared to answer tough questions from networking contacts and hiring authorities

Work out a fair separation plan

Develop a financial game plan

If you ever lose a job, as millions of Americans have in past twenty years, be prepared for the tough questions you will be asked once you implement your networking campaign. Also plan your finances carefully and work out an amicable and fair separation agreement from your employer.

I.   Answering tough questions about the loss of a job

A situation for which you should prepare yourself is answering awkward questions about your loss of a job. While it can be embarrassing, you must be prepared with answers that put you in a favorable light. First, be direct and answer the question immediately, preferably in the first sentence. Then "bridge" to positive ground by adding a comment about your excellent work history and/or your ability to provide specific benefits to a future company. Limit your answer to 2-5 sentences.

Below are some suggested approaches to handling frequently asked questions about the loss of a job.

Question: <u>Were you offered another position at the company</u>?

#1   Yes. The company suggested I could fill an open position in the graphic design department. I believe I can best meet my career potential by continuing to explore opportunities in marketing, opportunities that will take advantage of my experience and skills as a marketing manager. I was particularly effective in helping our marketing group translate focus group findings into the highlighting of consumer preferred product features in our advertising of Elite. I am confident I could provide similar insight for other products—all with an excellent eye for effective visual design in advertising, packaging and promotion.

Question: **Were you offered another position at the company? (cont.)**

#2 My position was eliminated during the corporate reorganization. All of Pro-Magnetics' sales are now being done by outside contract representatives. I know my supervisor opposed this decision because I had been so productive as an inside sales representative. I have cooperated fully in the transition and am sharing my best practices with the manager of the outside sales team.

Now I am seeking a challenging inside sales position that will take advantage of my outstanding product knowledge and telephone skills. I am particularly proud of my role in gaining new customers through a cold calling campaign I initiated and successfully implemented last year.

Question: **Were you replaced in this position?**

I understand a new college graduate was hired at an entry-level salary. I am looking at this situation as an opportunity to bring my broad experience and talents to another organization—one that values reliability, good interpersonal skills, and a dedication to realizing departmental and company goals.

Question: **Was someone else retained and you let go?**

A senior staff credit analyst was retained. I left Pro-Magnetics on good terms and am looking forward to making a strong contribution with another organization. For example, I will bring my ability to save time and money by simplifying credit checking procedures, something Pro-Magnetics appreciated.

Question **Were you asked to leave?**

Yes, much to my surprise. I can tell you that people familiar with my work will provide me with excellent references, as will supervisors at Royal Point Office Machines and Blue Ash Electronics. I have had an excellent record of helping cut costs and speed up reporting processes in their credit departments, efficiencies I am sure a number of organizations will value.

II. Finalizing your relationship with your present company

Confirm your terms of separation. Deal with your previous organization in as positive a manner as possible. It will be important for you to let nothing interfere with the positive attitude you need for a successful networking effort—and a positive attitude on your part is your best bet for getting company cooperation on issues such as the financial terms of your separation, aid in a job search, and getting an appropriate reference to use in your next job.

Get written confirmation of the following issues:

Financial settlement:
- separation pay
- bonuses;
- commissions;
- vacation pay

Insurance:
- period of time for which the company will pay your benefits;
- period of time and cost for which you may continue with company benefits at your own expense, such as life, medical, and hospital insurance
- availability of unemployment benefits

Aid in Job Search:

Ways company will agree to assist your future job search: references, referrals to potential employers, job search seminars, office facilities.

References:

- Write out a reason for your separation in as positive terms as possible

The statement might read something like this:

Harry's position was eliminated in a company-wide reorganization and we had no opening at the time which would use his skills.

- Ask your ex-supervisor if he or she would be comfortable making such a statement to any one who called asking to verify your reasons for separation.

If you get a "Yes," mail copy to the ex-supervisor.

If not, work out a positively phrased alternative on the phone and then send a copy of the ex-supervisor.

III.   Developing a financial game plan:

Your goal should be to stretch your income as far as possible: this way you will be in excellent financial condition if you find a job quickly, and you will also have a plan that will serve you well if your job search is extended. As a rule of thumb, in an average job market it takes 2-4 weeks for every $10,000 in income you expect to make.

First list all your sources of income, including your settlement payment, unemployment income, spousal income, and interest/dividends on investments. Then budget that money out over a worst case scenario—the longest period over which you believed you may be unemployed, such as 12 months.

Immediately develop a budget that will carry you through your job search. You want to be able to select a new job on its merits not on your financial need.

Account for every expense in writing. You will be surprised at how much money you spend and on what items.

Determine what expenses must be incurred, which can be reduced, and which can be eliminated until you have found a new position.

Necessary expenses	Expenses that can be reduced	Expenses that can be eliminated
Mortgage payments	Utilities	Restaurant meals
Medical Insurance	Credit card payments	Movies
Taxes	Grocery bills	Cable TV
Loans	Recreation	Magazines

Appendix IV
Leader's guide

Purpose of the leader's guide:

This guide was written both for teachers who will use the **Career Strategies** multimedia package as part of a college class and for professionals who intend to use these materials as a self study resource or in a continuing education seminar. Below I describe how to make the best use of Career Strategies materials, the rationale for using a multimedia approach to teaching employment skills, and options for using these materials when facilitating classes on organizing a networking and employment campaign.

How to make the best use this material:

Read the Table of Contents of the Career Strategies workbook. This will help you see the overall design of the book. **Career Strategies** contains eight chapters. It is organized so that each chapter builds on previously completed activities. The workbook contains numerous exercises that help seminar participants understand the power of networking as a way of finding jobs in the hidden job market; analyze what they want in a job; highlight what they have to offer employers; make out networking lists; write employment correspondence; and communicate effectively in networking and employment telephone calls and interviews.

Each chapter concludes with three types of exercises.

"Think About It" exercises are most appropriate for small group activity, where participants discuss their answers in small groups and learn from each other's experience.

The "Networking Activity" is designed as an after class activity to implement each of eight common networking practice.

"Three Things You Should Do Before You Read the Next Chapter" exercises are designed to get participants thinking about topics critical to understanding the materials covered in the subsequent chapter.

View the videotape. Narrated by Otis Williams, it is 24 minutes long and organized into four sections: what networking is and why it works; developing a networking data base; the networking telephone call; and the networking meeting.

Listen to Otis Williams' motivational audiotape on networking. It is approximately 40 minutes long, and it explains the power of networking as a skill critical to all aspects of a successful person's life. Its author and narrator, Mr. Otis Williams, won the Toastmaster's International Public Speaking contest in 1993. This tape, best offered as an after-class assignment, will help motivate participants to follow through on their networking commitments.

Visit each of the links on the www.careerstrategies.itp.com web site. These links will connect you with a host of materials on the World Wide Web, including excellent diagnostic tests, which can be taken and graded on-line. If possible, present the networking seminar in a computer lab, so you can incorporate these tests and other links into your teaching program. You will also find over 80 Power Point slides on this site which you can download and use as you discuss each chapter of the workbook.

Rationale for using a multimedia approach to learning: A multimedia approach to learning has numerous advantages. It encourages active learning, promotes retention, and allows students with differing learning styles to master the essentials of networking and employment campaigns.

Active learning: This program is based on Kolb's model of experiential learning and is designed to encourage active learning. Kolb observes that a person's *concrete experience* leads to *reflection* followed by *conceptualization* about the meaning of the experience which leads, to *active experimentation*, to see how the new understanding works in reality. Then the cycle begins anew, only this time with a changed perspective based upon previous learning. The **Career Strategies** materials are help lead students through this cycle to heighten their abilities to work productively in the Twenty-first Century.

> **Concrete experience**: Students see a videotape that explains the rationale for networking and demonstrates effective telephone and face- to-face networking. They also hear an audiotape with additional insight into the importance of networking to everyday life. They read the **Career Strategies** workbook and see Power Point slides that summarize the workbook's most important points about how to pursue opportunities in the "hidden job market." And they visit web sites that allow them to access extensive resources including tests for self analysis, information on target companies, and articles on a variety of employment issues.

> **Reflection**: Participants complete workbook and on-line graded tests and exercises which encourage them to reflect on how they can use their current knowledge of themselves, their job preferences, their work experiences, and their networks of friends, family, and colleagues to begin a successful job search campaign.

> **Conceptualization:** When they do the end-of-chapter "Think About It Exercises," students share their experiences with fellow participants and modify their thinking based on their interactions with others.

> **Active experimentation:** When students complete the "Networking Exercise" at the end of each chapter, they are actively testing the value of networking and proving to themselves that they can use networking to help them find the job of their dreams. The "Three Things You Should Do Before You Read the Next Chapter" exercises help focus student attention on key employment issues and activities that help them prepare for the next ideas introduced in the **Career Strategies** workbook.

Improved retention. A multimedia approach leads to outstanding retention. Research indicates that people learn best when all their senses are involved. For example, one study indicated that subjects remembered 70 per cent of what they saw, wrote, and said, compared to 10 per cent of what they read and 20 per cent of what they heard. This program allows participants to see networking in action, to hear about its value to career success, write down information that will build the foundation for effective networking, discuss their experiences with others, and practice written and oral communication skills critical to employment success.

Adapted to different learning styles.
programming research tells us that our population is roughly divided into three types of learners: visual, auditory, and kinesthetic—people who learn best by seeing, hearing, and acting respectively. A program that uses a video, Power Point slides, an audiotape, and hands-on activities will help all three groups effectively learn how to best find employment opportunities.

In addition, the out-of-class assignments used in the workbook and on the Web are well adapted to the differing amounts of time it takes students to grasp and master networking and employment search information.

209

Options for facilitating this tape

Option 1 (2 hours)

Introduce self and topic

set the stage by presenting info on value of networking; use accompanying Power Point slides

show the video, stopping to discuss the telephone interview and the face to face interview; use appropriate Power Point slides to facilitate discussion

ask group what key messages they got from the film

distribute copies of the workbook

review workbook exercises at end of Chapter One.

request that participants complete remaining workbook exercises as a self study give each participant an audio tape to listen to as review. Encourage participants to visit the website and access the resources linked to it.

Option 2 (3-4 hours)

Same as Option 1, plus have groups practice a networking phone call and a networking meeting in groups of 2-3. If 3 are in a group, rotate the roles of interviewer, interviewee, and observer.

Option 3 (all day)

Same as Option 2, only participants fill out selected workbook sheets in class, including networking prospects sheets. Have students discuss exercises in small groups. Students also practice telephone calls and networking meetings first in small groups and then in front of class.

Option 4 (five half-day sessions)

	Topic		Exercise
Day 1:	Chapters 1-2 in class	Job History	Record/discuss job history
Day 2:	Chapters 3-4	Self Assessment Networking Basics	Do assessment and networking exercises
Day 3:	Chapter 5-6	Networking Communication	Practice written and oral networking communication
Day 4:	Chapter 7	Employment Writing	Write job interview letters and e-mails
Day 5:	Chapter 8	Questions and Objections	Practice answering questions and objections

Option 5 (quarter or semester long class)

Use all materials and have students do all exercises. In my 10-week, two-credit class, I typically spend one week on Chapters 1-2; one week each on chapters 3-6; two weeks on chapter 7; and three weeks on chapter 8, including 7-10 minute job interviews by all students in front of the class.